Writing Successful Self-Help and How-To Books

Available at your local bookstore or with this coupon (cut out or photocopy).

Writing Successful Self-Help and How-To Books

Jean Marie Stine

John Wiley & Sons, Inc.

New York • Chichester • Weinheim • Brisbane • Singapore • Toronto

Copyright © 1997 by Jean Marie Stine
Published by John Wiley & Sons, Inc.

Library of Congress Cataloging-in-Publication Data:

Stine, Jean Marie.
    Writing successful self-help and how-to books / Jean Marie Stine.
      p.   cm. — (Wiley books for writers series)
    Includes bibliographical references.
    ISBN 0-471-03739-7 (pbk. : alk. paper)
    1. Authorship.   I. Series.
PN147.S795   1997
808'.02—dc20   96-26886

Printed in the United States of America

10 9 8 7 6 5 4

To Jeremy Tarcher
For ten wonderful years no girl could ever forget

Contents

Part Two
The Basics: Title and Outline

Part Three
Writing a Self-Help/How-To Proposal

Contents

Part Four
Writing the Sample Chapter

Acknowledgments

I want to express my gratitude to all the authors of self-help/how-to books I have been privileged to work with over the past quarter century. I learned far more from their aims, insights, solutions, and presentations than they ever learned from me. Without their manuscripts, and their efforts, this book would not exist.

Among the authors to whom I feel particularly indebted are Henry Wei, Ph.D.; John Klimo, Tina Tessina, Ph.D.; Timmen Cermak, Ph.D.; Beverly Engel, Ph.D.; Dion Dolphin, David Chamberlain, Ph.D.; and Patricia Matthews, Ph.D. Space does not permit listing the dozens of others who deserve equal acknowledgment. In repayment for all I learned from them, I can only express my heartfelt thanks.

I would also like to thank my colleagues at Houghton-Mifflin, St. Martin's, Newcastle, Jeremy P. Tarcher, and the Donning Company. These publishing professionals—from every level and department—were gracious enough to share with me over the years their insights into what makes a successful self-help/how-to book. Any success I might have had as a self-help/how-to editor is entirely due to their patience and generosity.

A very special thanks is due to my agent, Bert Holtje, whose council and encouragement helped bring this project to light. But, most of all, I owe a debt that can never be repaid to my extraordinarily patient editor, PJ Dempsey. She not only continually sharpened the focus and pacing of this book, but did yeowoman's duty, nursing its author through one of the most painful and prolonged crises of her life. Thanks are also due to John Cook who helped shepherd the book through the final stages of publication.

And a final thanks to Brenda Emily Burke for services rendered.

Introduction

If you are considering writing a self-help or how-to book—one that will help people solve tough personal problems or acquire important new skills—then this book is for you. In it you will find much valuable food for thought as well as a number of insider tips that you won't find elsewhere.

Many self-help/how-to authors prefer to write their books unassisted. Others don't have the time, or the language skills, to set their ideas down in book form themselves. Professional ghostwriters collaborate with them, to varying degrees, in the organizing, writing, and polishing of their material.

It doesn't make any difference who you are—a professional in the field you are writing about, a collaborator/coauthor, or even a ghostwriter. It doesn't even matter what kind of self-help or how-to book you plan to write. If your book offers readers practical strategies for acquiring skills or improving their lives—from "recovery" to effective management to building a kitchen cabinet—you will find everything you need to know here.

The guidance provided in this book is addressed directly to the self-help/how-to author. But the techniques detailed in its pages pertain equally to ghostwriters or collaborators who assist them with their books.

Anyone writing shorter, magazine- or newspaper-length self-help/how-to articles or columns will find that the ideas, advice, and instructions in this book apply to them, too. All the information about what to include in a book proposal, for instance, should be covered in much briefer form in a one- to two-page letter of inquiry. This letter should also detail your ideas and expertise and why you feel they are especially suited to the publication's readership, and ask whether the editor would be interested in reviewing your manuscript.

Other than that, the same principles that produce successful self-help/how-to books hold true for producing successful articles and columns, as well. No matter what the length of a manuscript, the rules—for outlining, style, headings, lists, quotations, references, illustrations, permissions, and other aspects of self-help/how-to writing—are identical. Just substitute "article" or "column" for the word "book" as you read through these pages.

I have spent over fifteen years as an editor specializing in self-help/how-to books. I've worked with hundreds of authors as well as ghosted more than a dozen such books for people who had important expertise they wanted to share with others. I have also been privileged to spend many hours discussing what makes a successful self-help/how-to book with knowledgeable editors and publishers. These experiences aided me in pinpointing pitfalls that can doom a novice's potential bestseller to obscurity. They also showed me how you can incorporate in your own manuscript many of the distinguishing qualities that send self-help/how-to books straight to the top of the bestseller lists.

In the following pages, I have distilled all of this information into a simple program that will lead you step by step through the successful production of your own self-help/how-to book.

Part One shows you how to use your credentials to sell your book with a simple proposal and writing sample.

Part Two tells you how to put together the basics of your book—the title and outline.

Part Three shares insider secrets for creating a successful proposal.

Part Four guides you through the basic components of a successful self-help/how-to chapter, from style through case histories and exercises.

Part Five introduces the Lazy Writer's system for editing your chapter once it's completed.

Part Six gives you tips on selling your proposal and getting your manuscript into professional form.

Part Seven shows shortcuts that pros use to make dealing with references, bibliographies, permissions, and illustrations a piece of cake.

I recently helped a clinical psychologist sell her first book. We prepared the proposal, as well as the sample chapters, using the exact procedures described in this book. It sold to the second publisher who saw the manuscript. At the moment, she is putting the finishing touches on her final chapter and eagerly looking forward to publication.

Now, it's your turn!

Part One

Writing and Selling
Self-Help/How-to Books

What You Should Know about Writing Self-Help/How-To Books

1.1 It's Easy, It's Rewarding—Do It!

Self-help/how-to books are easy to write. They enrich readers' lives. They are also financially rewarding.

Human beings are always in search of ways to resolve personal problems or expand their mental, physical, social, and professional skills. That keeps self-help/how-to books in constant demand. It keeps publishers on the constant lookout for them. And it makes writing them a wise investment in time and labor. When you have something new to offer or a powerful twist on established techniques, writing a self-help/how-to book can even result in riches and fame. (If you are one of those lucky individuals who doesn't need the money your book earns, the royalties can always be donated to a worthwhile cause.)

There are other rewards to writing a self-help/how-to book. There's the personal satisfaction that comes from helping readers. Whether your book is about healing troubled relationships, creating heirloom-quality quilts, or anything in between, there is nothing like the inner glow that stems from knowing you've contributed to the lives of others. Only self-help/how-to books convey this feeling, and nothing else compares to it.

Let's get back to that part about self-help/how-to books being easy to write. I'm not fooling. Writing a book might sound like a lot of work. In fact, for some authors it is a lot of work. But don't be daunted—it doesn't have to be.

When it comes to books, the old adage "work smarter, not harder" holds true. Why make it hard on yourself? Smart writers (in this case, lazy equals smart) have learned you don't have to strain to write a good book. They don't spend grueling hours locked away from family and friends. They take the low road, using tricks, secrets, and shortcuts to produce books in half the time. They don't cut corners on quality, either.

I have taken all those tricks, secrets, and shortcuts and turned them into a system that makes writing a self-help/how-to book a breeze. By breaking down each aspect of writing—from chapters to permissions—into a series of simple steps, I've made it so easy, you'll actually have fun along the way. Best yet, as you complete each step, you acquire skills you'll use in later sections of this book to write other parts of your book. By the time you reach the end, you will have acquired all the skills you need to write a quality self-help/how-to book.

I'm also going to show you how to sell your book before you write it—so publishers will actually be paying you to do the writing. That's right, *before* you write it! (You'll learn how and why in the next chapter.) A key strategy in this program is creating a proposal and sample chapter so you can sell your book before you write it. The focus is on taking you step by step through developing a proposal (Part Three) and a sample chapter (Part Four).

Then you'll learn to troubleshoot what you write using the Lazy Writer's Self-Editing Checklist (Part Five). After that, the focus is on how to submit and sell your proposal and sample chapter once you are satisfied that you have made them as strong as you can (Part Six). In the final section (Part Seven), you will discover shortcuts in dealing with permissions and front and back matter. The two appendixes provide lists of publications and organizations that can help.

1.2   Twenty-One Skills You Will Acquire from Reading This Book

I'm not kidding. Follow every step of my program and long before it's over you will have developed the twenty-one key skills needed to write a good self-help/how-to book:

1. Selling your book before you write it—and why you should.
2. Preparing your manuscript for submission to publishers.
3. Giving readers the three things they want most in a self-help/how-to book.
4. Creating bestseller titles and subtitles.
5. Writing a proposal that sells.
6. Organizing a bestseller outline.
7. Developing chapter titles that sell your book.
8. Getting your reader's attention by opening with a hook.
9. Crafting successful first and last chapters.
10. Developing a style that draws the reader.
11. Using nonsexist language and gender-neutral pronouns.
12. Making your pages user-friendly with headings, bullets, and other interactive elements.
13. Writing—and using—case histories.
14. Incorporating exercises, checklists, and self-quizzes.
15. Editing your first draft like a pro.
16. Placing material that doesn't seem to fit anywhere.
17. Correctly attributing quotations from others.
18. Effectively handling references, cross-references, footnotes, bibliographies, resources, and other components.
19. Dealing with permissions for quotations, photos, and illustrations.
20. Finding agents and publishers.
21. Presenting your manuscript to agents and publishers.

You'll have learned more than double this by the time you're through with the book.

1.3   Why Self-Help and How-To Books are Alike

Although self-help and how-to books might seem different on the surface, publishing professionals know the basics are the same. Both genres are practicality oriented: Both concentrate on helping people make improvements by teaching them new abilities, both provide specific step-by-step guidance in learning these abilities, and both provide examples and illustrations that make the book's techniques easier to use and understand.

Even if you have read other books on writing and attended writing workshops, you will find this book an invaluable resource. That's because self-help/how-to books are so unique. Because they are written to guide others through the implementation of new attitudes or skills—rather than just to inform or entertain—they have special needs most courses and books on writing fail to address. Other books, for example, don't need to have clear exercises, effective headings, checklists, and other interactive elements that play a vital role in heightening the effectiveness of self-help/how-to writing.

Different as they are from other genres, however, self-help/how-to books are very similar to each other. So when it comes to following the correct rules for writing one, whether your book is self-help or how-to doesn't matter. The mechanics of formatting a list, presenting an exercise, creating a heading, or handling references are the same. The only difference between self-help books and how-to books lies in their focus: Self-help books provide readers with the means to overcome critical problems or to achieve personal growth; how-to books guide others through the acquisition of specific skills.

1.4   How This Book Will Help You

Publishers estimate that dozens of self-help/how-to manuscripts by novice writers go unpublished for every one that sees print—despite the author's often impressive credentials. All of these unpublished manuscripts have something important to say. But their message goes unheard because the manuscripts are crippled by common, easily remedied mistakes.

Successful self-help/how-to books are the result of careful thought and preparation by experienced authors, ghostwriters, or editors. Publishing professionals know what makes these kinds of books bestsellers, and they put that knowledge to work for them to make their books a success.

By the time you finish this book, you too will have that knowledge. With it you'll avoid the mistakes that prevent many self-help/how-to manuscripts from being published. You'll also discover how easy it is to build the qualities that help readers make the most of your ideas.

Selling Your Self-Help/How-To Book Made Easy

2.1 One Chapter and a Short Proposal—All You Need to Sell Your Book

Want to know the simple trick professional writers use to sell their books? Just send a description of what your book will be like and a sample of your writing to a publisher. What could be easier than that?

Writing a book first and then selling it is hard work. But publishers are always on the lookout for self-help/how-to books written by those with expertise. They know people take a self-help/how-to book far more seriously when it is written by someone with personal knowledge of the subject—a doctor, for example. Reviewers, journalists, and talk-show hosts know this, too. A book by someone who fits this bill has a much better chance than one by a journalist who has merely researched the subject and only knows about it secondhand.

If you are reading this book, you are probably someone with just that kind of knowledge to share. If so, whether it comes from professional or personal experience, publishers will consider you to possess an important "credential" and be eager to read your book. If you do not feel you have a strong enough credential yourself, you can always consider contacting someone who does and asking that person to be your coauthor. (See Recommended Reading in the

Appendixes for information on Eva Shaw's *Ghostwriting: How to Get into the Business*.)

What qualifies as a credential to a publisher? Any involvement with a self-help or how-to subject area that gives you unique insights that could benefit others. Publishers, journalists, producers, talk-show hosts, readers, and audiences perceive you as an expert if, in the area you are writing about, you

- are a professional or well-credentialed amateur;
- have received a degree of any kind in the field or a closely allied area;
- possess a vital "insider's" skill (cabinet-making, recovery from addiction, improving your tennis score, plumbing, building a billion-dollar-a-year business, helping women achieve career success, making marriage work, painting large-scale murals, etc.);
- have edited publications on or specialized in writing about the field over a long period of time;
- possess some other form of expertise or special insight relevant to your subject.

If you—or the person you are collaborating with—meet any of these qualifications, then publishers will consider you to be credentialed in your field and your book a desirable addition to their list. More importantly, they will be willing to evaluate and purchase your book before you write it—based solely on a writing sample and short proposal.

2.2 Five Good Reasons to Sell Your Self-Help/ How-To Book before Writing It

Claiming that it's easy to sell publishers your book first and then get them to pay you to write it may sound like a pipe dream, but it's actually standard publishing practice—the way publishers buy most books. There are several reasons why it makes things easier for them and easier for you:

1. You put almost zero work (though a good deal of thinking) into your book before you sell it.
2. You get valuable publishing and editorial insights before you write the bulk of the manuscript.
3. If publishers don't respond, you can revise your approach (easier than a whole book) and submit again.
4. It helps publishers schedule books in advance.
5. It helps you plan and pursue the best strategy for writing your book.

2.2.1 Zero Work and Saved Time

Writing a book before you sell it has too many pitfalls. If it fails to sell, the time you have devoted to the effort—months, perhaps years— is wasted. Even if your book is accepted with revisions, hundreds of pages might have to be rewritten to gain publisher approval.

2.2.2 Publisher Input—Before Writing

Sometimes a publisher may like your ideas, but not your approach. Obviously, publishers feel more comfortable suggesting basic changes when you've only written a few pages, instead of an entire manuscript.

2.2.3 Two Chances at Success

If no publisher makes an immediate offer, read through the rejection letters. Revise your material with their criticisms in mind. Publishers are always willing to look at a revised book proposal. Although few outside the publishing industry know it, many major bestsellers only became bestsellers the second time around. The first time they were submitted, these books were rejected by everyone. But their savvy authors paid careful attention to the critiques and made extensive revisions with them in mind. Naturally, the same publishers found the revised proposal irresistible, because it now reflected exactly what they wanted in the book.

2.2.4 Publishing Schedules

The six months or a year you spend writing a book, after the publisher has contracted it, provides time for the publisher to develop effective marketing and promotion plans. Those plans must be in place six months prior to publication—so that bookstores can include your book in their yearly budget and the print and electronic media can schedule reviews and interviews.

2.2.5 The Best Strategy for Writing Your Book

You can develop every detail of your book before you start writing. In the course of writing your proposal and sample chapter, you'll

- precisely define your theme and audience;
- create a bestseller title;
- give your book irresistible reader (and sales) appeal;
- develop a best-selling style;
- find the best structure for your book, as well as for the individual chapters and subsections;
- present yourself as an expert whom publishers and the media will clamor to present.

You can see already how much easier accomplishing all this early on will make writing and selling your self-help/how-to book. Now you are ready to learn the easy way to submit your book to publishers.

Part Two

The Basics: Title and Outline

3

Finalizing Your Title and Subtitle

3.1 The Right Title Guarantees Success

Your proposal, like your book, begins with the title page. You may already have a title for your book that sounds like a sure-fire bestseller. But before typing the title page for your proposal, I want you to drop any preconceptions you might have. We're going to take a fresh look at the whole subject of titles. It's not possible to overstress the importance of this step.

It's no secret: The right title alone can make your book a success. In fact, some titles practically guarantee success. Think about *Women Who Love Too Much*, *Everything You Always Wanted to Know about Sex (but Were Afraid to Ask)*, *The 8-Week Cholesterol Cure*, and *Think and Grow Rich*.

Every woman who saw Robin Norwood's book felt she had loved too much at least once in her life. She was eager to see whether the book reflected her own experiences and curious to find what light it might shed on her own romantic entanglements. The result: Millions of women picked up *Women Who Love Too Much* and made it a bestseller.

Tens of millions of men and women felt compelled to glance at David Rubin's book (*Everything You Always Wanted to Know about Sex*) once they saw the title. Their interest piqued, they were anxious to discover whether there was really anything important they didn't already know about sex.

People across the world wanted to know how they could lower their cholesterol to healthier levels in a mere eight weeks. Everyone expects quick results these days. By promising readers that the cure would take only eight weeks, *The 8-Week Cholesterol Cure* sold millions of copies for its author.

Or take Napoleon Hill's fabulous four-decade-long flirtation with the bestseller lists. No one who sees the title *Think and Grow Rich* can resist leafing through its pages and ultimately purchasing the book. We all want to know whether we can achieve our dreams of wealth simply by thinking rich.

3.2   The Billboard for Your Book

One of the most important steps in selling your self-help/how-to book to publishers is developing a title no reader can resist. When you have a title readers can't resist, publishers won't be able to resist it, either.

The first thing a reader notices about your book is the title. It's a billboard—or advertisement—for your book. Your title should stop people in their tracks and make them take your book off the shelf for a closer inspection. When it does, you are 90 percent of the way to persuading them to take it home and give your ideas a try.

3.3   You, Too, Can Create a Bestselling Title

It's a well-kept secret in the publishing industry that great titles often aren't born of the author's inspiration—they're made from the sweat of the author, publisher, and others working in tandem. Often, dozens, sometimes literally hundreds, of titles are generated and discarded before everyone agrees that—bingo!—the perfect title has been found. That's what happened with *Women Who Love Too Much* and *DOS for Dummies*.

Creating a self-help/how-to title with instant success written all over it might seem like a special talent only some lucky individuals have. But there's a simple, three-step process—similar to the one publishers go through—that you can use to develop irresistible titles. Apply this strategy to all your books, and you can formulate winning titles every time.

Just as the focus in self-help and how-to books is different, so is the focus in their titles. Self-help titles are more promise-oriented; how-to titles aim at being informative. Self-help titles would include *What to Expect When You're Expecting* and *Chicken Soup for the Soul*; how-to titles would be *Woodworking Made Easy* and *The Internet Navigator*.

When following the instructions in this chapter for generating winning titles, look for promise-oriented titles if you are writing a self-help book or descriptive, informative titles if you are writing a how-to book.

3.4   What Makes an Irresistible Title?

Look over the titles I used as examples: *Women Who Love Too Much*, *Everything You Always Wanted to Know about Sex (but Were Afraid to Ask)*, *Think and Grow Rich*, and *The 8-Week Cholesterol Cure*. Each title is distinctive—so distinctive that it practically entered the language as a phrase. Each sums up its book's self-help/how-to message and theme in a few potent, evocative words. Capture what is distinctive about your book in a short, pithy phrase, and you will be well on your way to a bestselling title.

Each of the preceding titles also contains additional qualities that helped to ensure instant success:

- Identifies a problem or lack the reader has.
- Makes a promise.
- Offers hope.
- If how-to, is practical and descriptive.

In the next section, these elements form the basis of a three-step process for generating titles.

3.5   How to Generate a Bestselling Title

Here's how to develop, troubleshoot, and perfect titles and sub-titles.

3.5.1   Identify a Problem or Lack

Make your title "click" with a problem that readers have or a skill they need; then they will have to look inside, eager to see what kind of help your book offers. Diverse as they are, each title cited in the preceding section identifies a problem or desire that millions of people have. The title *Women Who Love Too Much* singles out a problem most women feel they have suffered from at some time or other. The title *Everything You Always Wanted to Know about Sex* pinpoints the sexual embarrassment that holds us back from learning many things about sex that we desperately want to know. The title *Think and Grow Rich* promises to teach a vital skill that everyone wants. So does the title of the perennial *How to Win Friends and Influence People*. Who wouldn't like to have more friends and get what he or she wants from others without fuss or hassle?

Take out a sheet of paper (or open a computer file):

a. Write down the problem your book helps readers solve or the skills it will help them develop.
b. Be as specific as possible. Ask yourself the following: Are you writing about heart problems in general or only about those that concern people at high risk? Are you writing about financial success, personal success, or both? Are you teaching crocheting or how to crochet afghans?

3.5.2   Make a Promise

People who are in distress, or are seeking to expand their abilities, are focused on results. Make certain your title lets potential readers know you promise results that will make a difference in their lives. They won't be able to resist peeking inside your book to find out whether you will be able to fulfill that promise and how you will do it.

All of the titles mentioned in this chapter contain a promise that reading the author's book will benefit the reader in some major way. Most of the time this promise is explicit: "grow rich," "influence people," or learn "everything you always wanted to know about sex." Sometimes it is implied: *Women Who Love Too Much* suggests that female readers will learn about a common syndrome—and about its cure.

On the same sheet of paper (or in the same computer file):

a. Write down the promise you feel your title makes.
b. Try to capture specifically what you believe the book promises readers. What will it do to help improve the reader's life?

3.5.3 Offer Hope

There is a third factor you need to consider if you want an irresistible title: hope! People who come to a book seeking help or skills bring the hope that they can grow and improve. When your title speaks to that longing, readers respond positively to your book.

Just look at the hope offered in the titles of the five preceding bestsellers. "Grow rich" holds out the expectation of ending financial need. "Everything you always wanted to know" speaks to the hope that we will be sexually more knowledgeable (and presumably more fulfilled). Dale Carnegie's title *Win Friends and Influence People* promises both friendship and the ability to influence others in such a way as to make our lives easier, our endeavors more successful. *Women Who Love Too Much* may not seem to offer hope at first glance, but, as with its promise, the hope is there—it is merely implied. In this case, it is every woman's dream of a life in which she receives as much love from a mate as she gives.

On the same paper (or in the same computer file):

a. Describe the hope your book offers readers.
b. Be specific. What will the reader's life be like after your book has delivered on its promise?

Save your answers. You will need them in the next section when you finalize your title and later in this chapter. In Part Three, when you actually start writing the proposal for your book, you will also refer to your answers.

3.5.4   Be Informative (How-To Books)

How-to titles are straightforward. They describe exactly what the book is about. People seeking how-to books are looking for specific categories for specific kinds of help. Someone who wants to build birdhouses, crochet an afghan, learn accounting, or write a self-help/how-to book will grab the first book whose title proclaims it is about exactly that.

They would reach immediately for a book called *Birdhouse Building Made Simple*, *Crocheting the Perfect Afghan*, *Learn Accounting in Thirty Days!*, or *Writing Self-Help/How-To Books: A Step-by-Step Guide*. Each title instantly informs the reader what the book teaches and describes its subject clearly. Strive for this kind of directness when yours is a how-to book.

For how-to books, add this final step on the same sheet of paper (or in the same computer file):

a. Describe the specific ability your book teaches.
b. Strive for a title that will inform the reader—in a single glance—specifically what the book is about.

3.6   Finalizing the Title for Your Book

Put my book down for a few minutes (overnight, if you need to sleep on it) and concentrate on the title for your book.

Take the answers you generated to the questions in the preceding sections and incorporate them in half a dozen to a dozen potential titles for your book. You can even include your pet title now and any variants.

Keep your titles short and readable—under ten words, preferably under six. Short phrases have more punch—they are also easier to remember.

Also try to give each title a distinctive, attention-getting quality. Make a dramatic statement or an irresistible promise, like *How to Make $1,000,000 per Year during the Coming Recession*, or *Throw Away Your Glasses—Forever!*, or *It's Never Too Late for Love*.

3.6.1 How Professionals Look at Titles

By the time you begin reading this sentence you should have drawn up a list of several titles you think have potential. But even if you don't like any of the titles you have generated, that's okay, too. Writers and editors frequently put the elements of great titles together out of the pieces of rejects.

Let's try your titles against a preliminary test. If any of them meets the following criterion, you are already 90 percent of the way to a successful title. The following is taken directly from the writers' guidelines of a major international publishing firm.

> *The Title:* This should describe the theme of the book. The specific subject area covered must be evident from the title. Examples: *The Art of the Leader, Eating Better, Thinking Better, Four Steps to Power Crocheting, Sinus Survival*.

Glance over your own list of titles. Are there any that make it clear what the "specific subject area covered" in your book is? Of course there are. There have to be because you created them by combining elements from your answers to the guidelines in the preceding section. Give yourself a pat on the back. You have already learned how to dream up titles that meet the criterion set by one of the world's largest publishing companies.

3.6.2 The Self-Help/How-To Title Checklist

The following checklist contains a number of qualities publishing professionals believe go into making a winning self-help/how-to title. Compare each of your own titles, one at a time, against this list. Score one point for every "yes" you give to the following questions about each prospective title you have devised. The more points a title scores, the higher it rates.

☐ Is your title specific?

Does it say *Make Money from Home* when you mean *Make Money in the Home Mail-Order Business*?

☐ Is your title attention grabbing?

Is your title flat and boring, like *The Encyclopedia of Sex*, or catchy and exciting, like *Everything You Always Wanted to Know about Sex*?

☐ Is your title upbeat and positive?

Does your title dwell on the negative or neutral, like *Being Lonely and Ignored*, or does it emphasize the positive, like *Finding Your Ideal Mate*?

☐ Does your title offer the reader benefits?

Does your title simply say *A Financial Guide to the Coming Recession*, instead of promising readers *How to Make $1,000,000 per Year*?

☐ Will readers know what you mean?

Does the title use obscure terms, like *Codependency and Intimacy: A Female Perspective*, or is it stated in language anyone can recognize, like *Women Who Love Too Much*?

☐ Is your title short?

Will it be easy to say and remember? Only two of the bestselling titles in this chapter are longer than seven words, and they are easy to say.

Total up the scores for each title. You should probably discard any title that earned only three points or less. Save the rest. Publishers like getting one main title suggestion and two or three alternatives that the author also feels might be appropriate.

You now have several potential titles for your book as good as any generated by publishing insiders—plus a method for generating chapter, heading, and article titles any time you are stuck in the future.

3.7 The Words below the Title: Subtitles, Reading Lines, Shopping Lists

Don't stop with a title. Create flair and boost reader appeal by amplifying your theme with a few descriptive, eye-catching words below the title.

You've probably noticed that most bestselling self-help/how-to books have both a title and a descriptive phrase or two below or following it. This phrase further develops the title, as in *The Thirteenth Step: Finding Independence, Self-Reliance and Autonomy beyond the Self-Help Programs.*

3.7.1 Subtitles

A well-chosen subtitle will enhance your book's chances for success by tipping readers off to key benefits or a unique approach.

If your book's main emphasis is on practical help and benefits, base your subtitle on those elements. That's what the authors of these bestselling titles did: *Smart Love: Changing Painful Patterns,*

Choosing Healthy Relationships; *Pregnancy and Dreams: How to Have a Peaceful Pregnancy by Understanding Your Dreams*; and *How to Be Twice as Smart: Boosting Your Brainpower and Unleashing the Miracles of Your Mind.*

One excellent reason for highlighting your book's benefits is that it will be competing in the same marketplace as other "feel-good" products. Make readers aware that they are getting a substantial, long-term value from the money they invest in your book and that purchasing it is a bargain they can't afford to pass up.

Or perhaps what distinguishes your book from others is a particular approach or slant that you have developed over the years. Capture what is unique about your approach on the cover in a cleverly worded subtitle, and people will feel challenged to take your book home and try your system for themselves. The subtitle on one recent book tells it all: *A Codependence Recovery Program Based on Relationship Addiction Support Groups.* Here's another: *Peak Performance Techniques of the Russian and East German Olympic Victors.* Or *A Self-Help Guide to Allergies, Bronchitis, Colds and Sinusitis.* A last example: *The Twelve-Steps & Management.* The great advantage of this type of subtitle is that all the readers looking for the approach you take, or the kind of system you use, will know in an instant that your book is for them.

3.7.2 Reading Lines

When what you have to say is a little too long to fit comfortably in a subtitle, you may have a *reading line.* A reading line is longer than a subtitle—other than that the distinction is moot.

The point is that you don't have to feel constrained by what you think of as a reasonable length for a subtitle. Let the phrases you put below your title be as long as you need them to be. That's what this author did when she and her publisher came up with the reading line "A Parent-Guided Program for Children of All Ages Who Can't, Won't, or Haven't Yet Started to Read." A mouthful, certainly—but one that would never have had the same impact on its intended audience if it had been cut by even one word.

Or consider one of my favorite reading lines: "Techniques for Getting through Loss, Setbacks, Upsets, Disappointments, Difficulties, Trials, Tribulations, and All That Not-So-Funny Stuff." Too long for a subtitle, too humorous to be taken as a list of benefits, this book has sold tens of thousands of copies for my friend Allen Klein under the title *The Healing Power of Humor*.

When you feel that to really put across to the reader what your book is about you need a long string of words under the title, start thinking in terms of a reading line.

3.7.3 Shopping Lists

Sometimes your book has too many benefits to capture in a subtitle or reading line. When that happens, use what publishers call a *shopping list* on the cover. This may sound trite, but you actually see it all the time, particularly on self-help/how-to books. A shopping list is simply a list, usually bulleted, of important benefits the reader will receive from your book, such as the following:

- Information the reader will learn
- Skills that will be acquired
- Problems that will be solved
- Illnesses that will be cured or helped
- Conditions or situations that will be improved

One recent bestseller, *Mastering the Information Age*, offered modern executives a cluster of vital skills needed to keep up with the information flood created by modems, CD-ROM, faxes, and the Internet. The book highlighted many of these skills on the cover, offering readers a tantalizing sampler of all the ways it could improve their lives. Among them were the following:

- Get control of your information overload.
- Learn to read faster and plow through books, reports, and memos.
- Quickly find the information you need.
- Remember more facts and data.
- Think more sharply.
- Achieve your peak intelligence.

When you have a lot to offer, let readers know it. Add a shopping list under the title. All those benefits show readers just how much they need your book—it's like writing your own personal ticket to bestsellerdom.

3.7.4 Picking Your Descriptive Phrase

a. Write down elements that you feel aptly capture important points of your book.
b. Go wild—the more the merrier.
c. Use the Self-Help/How-To Title Checklist (in Section 3.6.2) to finalize your choice.

3.8 *Troubleshooting*

Here's how to troubleshoot your title, subtitle, reading line, and shopping list. Even if you are satisfied with what you have, I want you to take one last but all-important step. Try out your prospective title and subtitle on some potential readers—in this case, friends, business associates, or anyone you think intelligent and sympathetic.

It's the visual appeal of your title and subtitle you want to test. There is a big difference between the aural and visual senses (consider the phrase "seeing is believing"). So print out your title ahead of time, by typewriter, computer, or by hand—it doesn't matter. Inform the people you're consulting that you are writing a book and would like their opinion on a potential title and subtitle. Hand them the sheet, let them read it, and then get their reaction.

Here's a final, all-important tip: If you want a 100 percent unbiased response, include several of your discarded titles and subtitles (or reading line or shopping list). Don't let anyone know which combination you have selected. This way you avoid unconsciously biasing acquaintances in favor of the title and subtitle you think are best.

If more people select the discards than the title and subtitle (or reading line or shopping list) that you have selected, then it's time to do some serious rethinking. Ask your friends what they liked about the title combination they chose. Ask them what they didn't like about the one you preferred.

Revise your title, subtitle, or reading line or shopping list in light of what you have learned. Try them on a fresh set of acquaintances. When you achieve unbiased accord, you'll be ready to set up the title page of your proposal.

3.9 Formatting Your Title Page

Fire up your typewriter or computer and begin your title page:

1. Type your name and address in the upper left-hand corner of the page.
2. About three inches down, center the title and subtitle.
3. Under this, type the word "Proposal."
4. Follow that with your name again, along with any degrees or other distinctions.

Slip in a clean sheet, or open another computer file. Now that your title is finalized, it's time to turn to the proposal's outline.

4

Outlining a Self-Help/ How-To Book

4.1   *How a Chapter Outline Helps Write Your Book*

A detailed table of contents for your book, presented in *chapter outline* form, is a must in any proposal. This detailed, chapter-by-chapter plan for your book should list major topics and subtopics (see Chapter 10). This chapter outline (sometimes called an *annotated* or *expanded table of contents*) tells publishers many important things about your book. It shows them that the overall shape and progression of your book are sound. It gives them a preview of your major ideas and exercises. It helps editors guide the sales and marketing department (who seldom read the complete proposal) straight to the meat of your book.

A detailed chapter outline is also an enormous help to you when you sit down to start writing. If you have prepared a detailed plan of each chapter with its sections and subsections, more than half your work as a writer is done already. You merely fill in the blanks.

Developing a detailed outline of your book can save you wasted effort and unnecessary frustration. It can help you organize ideas more clearly; pinpoint extraneous, underdeveloped, and misplaced material; and reveal other weak areas in your plan for the book.

Developing a chapter outline will help spark new ideas, suggest elements you should include in your book, and give you a rough idea of the proportion of theory to practical exercises. When you have finished this chapter, you will be able to outline like a pro and instantly troubleshoot your own chapter outline for flaws.

Even if you have already drawn up an outline for your book, you should still read this chapter because it includes insider tips for constructing winning book outlines. That way, you can be sure that your outline includes all the elements publishing professionals believe spell "bestseller" when you are finally ready to submit your proposal.

4.2 The Five Ways of Structuring a Self-Help/ How-To Book

Each of the five basic types of self-help/how-to books comes with its own "built-in" chapter outline. Identify which type your book is, and follow the appropriate outline format.

The five kinds of self-help/how-to books are referred to by insiders as follows:

1. The programmatic or step-by-step book
2. The recovery book (self-help only)
3. The evolutionary book
4. The component-based book
5. The exercise-based book

4.2.1 The Programmatic Book

Does your book center around a specific system for solving a reader's problem, by teaching new skills or improving his or her life? Is it as much how-to as self-help? If so, you have a ready-made chapter outline based on the elements of your program. By basing each chapter on a stage or step in your system, you develop a winning outline with little effort.

One diet expert's program provided her with all the basic elements she needed to outline her bestseller:

- Charting your eating profile
- Taking control of your eating patterns
- Making your home a fat-free zone
- Feeding your body—not your feelings
- Making your home off-limits to eating
- Learning to "go hungry"
- Discovering your new body

With a few modifications, she had the material for what became the seven core chapters of her book.

In a book on building birdhouses, another author devoted a chapter to each step in the process:

- Designing the house
- Building the floor
- Building the walls
- Building the roof
- Cutting out the door
- Assembling the floor and walls
- Assembling the roof

Use this same programmatic, step-by-step approach for books on

- Success
- Developing skills
  Professional and personal
  Do-it-yourself
  Self-improvement
  Athletics, sports, and fitness
- Resolving personal problems
- Diet and health

4.2.2　The Recovery Book (Self-Help Only)

Does your book tell readers how they can enter recovery from addictive or compulsive behaviors? Count yourself lucky, as these books are the easiest to outline. Most recovery books center around the classic 12 steps of Alcoholics Anonymous. Some present the reader with fewer steps—seven- and ten-step programs are common. These steps form a ready-made chapter outline just waiting to be filled in. Each step becomes a jumping-off point for a chapter. In this respect, recovery books sound similar to books based on programmatic elements, but there are critical differences.

Readers entering recovery or those already in recovery have special needs. People struggling with addictive/compulsive behaviors, for instance, may suffer from denial, or they may be unsure about having the problem your book addresses and have bought the book to see if, in fact, they are sufferers. Help them determine if they belong to the group the book is written for. Present a checklist of symptoms or a self-quiz. Use a heading like "Are You a Substance Abuser?" or "Six Signs of Compulsive Gambling."

4.2.3　The Evolutionary Book

Does your book center on the stages through which a problem or skill develops over a period of time? If so, take the evolutionary approach to structuring your book. You might be telling your own story, of how over a number of years, through a series of turning points, you continually deepened your understanding of the subject of the book, finally leading you to the insights that form the basis of your method or ideas. Or you could be describing how the reader's own psychological or physical problems evolved. When your book deals with an evolving process, organize each chapter around one of the stages in that process.

Conversely, you might be writing about the evolutionary steps every carpenter goes through in learning his or her skill. If so, you would build each chapter around one of those stages.

Let's say your book is on corporate evolution. It charts the eight stages companies pass through as they grow from a small new firm to a giant multinational conglomerate. You offer insights for managers on how they can successfully navigate the challenges of each stage. Develop the core of your chapter outline by devoting a chapter to each stage—along with exactly how to overcome the challenges it presents.

4.2.4   The Component-Based Book

Does your book show people how to cope with the individual parts of a problem—or the individual steps involved in acquiring a new ability? When a process is long term or complex, tackle it one component at a time.

Your book might be on motivation for athletes, businesspeople, and others. The main components of the "winning attitude" might be the following:

- Wanting to win
- Setting a goal
- Visualizing yourself winning
- Tuning out the world
- Surrendering yourself to the moment

Or you might be writing about using the home computer for a successful job search. The main components might be the following:

- Writing and formatting cover letters on your computer
- Searching for leads on the Internet
- Establishing a personal World Wide Web page
- Accessing career-specific mailing lists and business-to-business yellow pages on CD-ROM discs

In a book on copyediting, one author arranged her book around such skills as the following:

- Marking the page
- Using copyediting symbols
- Looking for misspellings
- Looking for improper punctuation
- Attributing sources
- Checking facts

When organizing the components, relax. You'll find that the chapter outline essentially organizes itself.

4.2.5 The Exercise-Based Book

Is your program concerned primarily with developing skills, rather than theory and background? If so, focus your approach on leading readers through practical exercises and techniques. In a book on recovery from relationship addiction, some exercises might guide the reader through letting go of an obsession with another person, some through nurturing oneself, some through defining boundaries, some through learning how to make choices, and some through developing a capacity for healthy intimacy. By merely gathering exercises of a similar nature together in chapters, you have a ready-built chapter outline.

4.3 Five Shortcuts to Better Outlines

You probably saw your book and its basic chapter outline in the preceding section. But if you didn't—or even if you did—I am going to show you five quick shortcuts that veteran writers use to turn out winning chapter outlines in minutes. Use these same shortcuts to outline chapters, sections, and subsections:

1. List the main points you want to make.
2. Look for missing elements.
3. Look for similar elements—and reorganize.

4. Look for main themes and minor themes—to develop chapters.
5. Make use of your leftovers.

4.3.1 List the Main Points You Want to Make

Successful outlines are organized around a book's main points. These points provide a framework, which makes the actual writing of the book a great deal easier. Jot down what seem the most important ideas, steps, techniques, or skills you want to share with your readers.

4.3.2 Look for Missing Elements

Review your starter list. Are any elements missing? Seeing your ideas written down usually provokes other notions that amplify on those or fill in missing gaps. Add any new ideas that this review sparks.

To make certain you don't miss anything, show your list to friends. Ask them whether there is anything missing that they would expect to find, or like to see, in a book on your subject. (This technique was suggested by an editor-in-chief who swore it helped authors spot important holes they overlooked.)

4.3.3 Look for Similar Elements—and Reorganize

When you are reasonably sure you have listed most of your key points, look for similar elements. As you gather together material on similar themes, find labels for each grouping. Review these groupings. Look for relationships among the overall themes.

Do any of these groups seem to belong together? If so, revise your list so that related sections are adjacent to each other. If different groups are similar enough, you might even want to combine them into a single group, under a single label.

4.3.4 Look for Main Themes and Minor Themes to Develop Chapters

With similar ideas grouped together, put a star by those you believe are important enough to warrant chapters of their own. If you seem to have too many (over twenty-five), try combining some of them. If you have too few (under five), try breaking a few into two or three chapters.

4.3.5 Make Use of Your Leftovers

As with any good dish, you may have leftover ingredients—important ideas and issues that don't seem to fit in with any of your major chapters or groupings. Ending up with material like this is a normal part of the writing process. It's a signal indicating that there is something distinctive about the ideas involved.

The first question to ask yourself is whether the material even belongs in your book. You may find you have tried to cram too much into one book and can readily do without it. If you are satisfied it belongs in the book, consider making it an appendix. Material that is vital to your book but that doesn't seem to go anywhere is often ideal appendix material. (You will discover much more about how to handle appendixes and what goes into them in Chapter 22.) Or consider showcasing this material in a concluding chapter, one that deals with matters that people might want to know after finishing all the preceding chapters.

4.4 Outlining Your First and Last Chapters— A Special Art

Here's how to organize first and final chapters: In the first chapter, summarize your book and motivate readers to give your ideas a try. In the last chapter, bring your book to a meaningful conclusion.

4.4.1 The First Chapter—Hooking Readers with a Preview

Before reading a book, most people will dip into the opening chapter to sample your wares. They are curious about the approach you take, the benefits you promise, and the book's overall feel. Satisfy this curiosity in your first chapter, and readers will keep on reading.

The first chapter should establish what your book is about and what readers can expect to learn. Only then should you present the first step of your system, the initial exercises, or an explanation of critical points. Your preview prevents readers from becoming confused and disoriented. The connection between what you present and their own lives "clicks" when people have an overall view of your approach and theme clearly in mind.

Some people decide whether to purchase your book based solely on skimming your first chapter. Preview your book in a way that conveys the excitement of your approach, promise, and ideas, and potential readers will feel it's a must-have. Boil down your entire book and its key points to the length of a good magazine article, and you have an ideal first chapter.

There are two other critical reasons for providing an overview of your book in the initial chapter. Many people who buy your book will never read anything else! Surveys show that up to one-half of a book's readers never go any farther than the first chapter. They dip into it to get the book's basic thrust and then put it down satisfied.

Other readers will skim your first chapter to pick up your book's overall theme and thrust and then skip directly to whatever chapters interest them most. Without such an overview, however, they gain no real sense of how to use those chapters.

4.4.2 The First Chapter Checklist

Adapted from one publisher's guidelines, the following is a short checklist of what a good first chapter should tell readers.

☐ What is the book about? (Amplify the theme stated in the title.)

☐ Why was the book written (very briefly), or what are the problems, skills, and solutions that it provides that other books don't?

☐ For whom is the book written?

☐ What makes this book different?

☐ Precisely how will the book confer its benefits on the reader—through preview steps, exercises, or attitudes?

☐ What benefits will the reader receive?

☐ What is the overall structure of the book or progression of the chapters?

When the time comes, putting your first chapter together won't be much trouble, because you will have already generated many of its ideas in the overview to your proposal (see Chapter 6).

4.4.3 The Last Chapter—Bringing Your Book to a Successful Conclusion

Just as an opening chapter should precede the first step of your program, the final chapter should follow the last step. This chapter doesn't have to be long, although, if you have a lot to say, it can be.

The trick is to round off your book and give the readers a strong send-off when they have finished, rather than just let the book end with the last step of your program.

You can use your final chapter to bring your book to a conclusion. This may be as simple as reiterating the key points you want readers to "take home with them" after finishing your book. If so, just outline in a few words those points.

Or you might wish to inspire the reader to take the steps your book offers by painting a picture of what life will be like for them when they have. If so, list the essential qualities of that life.

Your final chapter can also be a catchall for ideas and material that don't fit comfortably anywhere else. If so, outline these final thoughts.

Or maybe through experience you know there are questions that people will have before or after trying your program. If so, make these potential questions your final chapter. The question-and-answer format is very simple. Write each question as a new paragraph and underline it. In the next paragraph write the answer. Then write the next question.

4.5 Finalizing Your Chapter Outline

After organizing your tentative book chapters by topic, it's time to break down each chapter into sections and subsections.

4.5.1 Organizing a Chapter into Sections

Write a list of topics associated with the chapter. Put a checkmark by those you feel represent major themes or sections. If you are writing a chapter on the biology of depression, your main subjects might include issues such as the psychobiology of depression, the brain and depression, and the body and depression.

Reorganize the chapter to reflect your main sections. Use the following checklist to troubleshoot your chapter outline.

☐ Are there any sections listed that really don't belong in this chapter?

☐ Are there any duplications that should be eliminated?

☐ Are any important ideas missing?

If you answer yes to any of these questions, make a final reorganization of your book's main sections.

4.5.2   Organizing Your Sections into Subsections

Look at your sections. You will probably have several subthemes within each section. Within the brain and depression section, you might plan to write about the chemical balance of the healthy optimistic brain, how altering this balance causes depression, and the six factors that throw off this balance. Then go through the preceding checklist to troubleshoot your subsections.

You can apply the same process to identifying subsections within subsections (called sub-subsections). In a subsection about the six factors that throw off the brain's natural balance, you might have sub-subsections detailing elements of each factor. Dividing your book into sub-subsections is usually enough, but if you find that you need to break down sub-subsections, or even sub-sub-subsections, by all means do so.

4.6   Secrets of Irresistible Chapter Titles, Headings, and Subheadings

When creating your book's title (Chapter 3), you also developed the skills you need for devising attention-getting titles for your chapters and arresting headings for their sections.

As with your book's title and subtitle, the right chapter titles can play a major role in winning readers for your book. Otherwise, publishers and successful authors would just number their chapters and leave it at that. The table of contents is one of the first places prospective readers look. Good chapter titles alone can be enough to persuade a reader to take your book home. Titles reveal your overall structure—programmatic, recovery, evolutionary, or component- or exercise-based. They also tell the reader about promises and benefits. Chapter titles can also suggest a great deal about your own personal approach to your subject matter—serious, humorous, pragmatic. As with your book title, your chapter titles can be humorous, poetic, or whatever you would like them to be—as long as they are somehow descriptive of the chapter's subject matter or theme.

The chapter titles and headings you come up with now don't have to be perfect, so don't spend too much time on them or let composing them unduly delay you. You have already absorbed enough of the tricks of the trade to do a solid job and that's all that's required now. You can perfect them later, as you are writing your book. Publishers know that chapter and heading titles are only tentative at this point and subject to change. As long as your chapter titles and headings tell a bit about what the chapters and sections will contain and are lively, it shows you are aiming in the right direction. That is all publishers want to know.

To get you started, five different approaches to developing winning chapter titles follow. (We are discussing chapter titles here, but you can use the same methods for chapter headings and subheadings. Later, in Chapter 10, you will find an entire section devoted to special tricks for generating exciting headings that will lure the reader through your chapters.)

4.6.1 Descriptive Titles

Devise chapter titles that clearly reflect their subject matter. "How to Build a Support Network at Work," "The Six Signs of Compulsive Spending," and "Step 4: Teaching Your Dog to Heel" are typical examples. Make your titles lively, intriguing, and dramatic and still be descriptive. This way they won't sound clinical or academic, misleading readers to believe the book is for professionals.

4.6.2 Titles That Reflect Your Approach

Devise chapter titles that tell the reader something about your approach. If yours is a light-hearted look at marital difficulties, signal this to your prospective audience with light, humorous chapter titles.

If you are writing about resolving common marital problems, consider titles such as "I'm Right, You're Wrong—And That's the End of It" and "Fights—Fair and Unfair." If you want to offer warmth and support to those in pain, construct titles that reflect this: "Healing Your Inner Child," "Beyond Victimhood," "You Can Love Again," or "New Hope for Lasting Peace." If your book is pure how-to, with a focus on practical steps, you can reach your potential audience with chapter titles that center on the concrete elements of your program: "Learning to Purl," "Writing Your Resume," "Discovering Erogenous Zones."

4.6.3 Two-Part Titles: The Best of Both Worlds

You can devise chapter titles that are both descriptive and intriguing by using two-part titles. Think of these as a chapter title and subtitle.

One fledgling self-help/how-to author submitted clinical-sounding chapter titles like "Childhood in an Alcoholic Family," "Co-dependence and the ACA," and "Treatment for ACAs." Naturally, they made his book sound as if it might be meant for professionals in the field of alcoholic recovery, yet the book's title (*A Time to Heal*) and the book itself were warm and inviting, and the writing was aimed at anyone suffering from the effects of having been raised in an alcoholic family. His publisher solved the dilemma with two-part chapter titles, the first half poetic and the second descriptive: "A Time to Feel—Post-Traumatic Stress and the ACA," "A Time for Courage—Treatment for ACAs," and so on.

Also, use two-part titles to deepen the reader's understanding of your chapter's subject material. Examples include "Women in the Forbidden Zone: Stages in the Betrayal of Hope," "Daydreams, Storytelling, and Self-Discovery: How Our Daydreams Reflect Who We Are," "Constructing the Ship's Sails: The Miracle in the Bottle," and "Meeting the Athlete Within: Exercises for Tapping the Deep Unconscious."

4.6.4 Keep it Specific

Devise chapter titles that are specific rather than general. Specific titles make readers believe that they can successfully accomplish what your book teaches. State your case in a way that calls your reader to action, such as "Overcome the Fear of Public Speaking."

4.6.5 Put the Reader in Your Chapter Titles

Readers want to feel you are writing for them personally and that they are the subjects of your book. You can't go wrong with readers when you write them into your chapter titles. Chapter titles like "Unleashing Your 'Inner' Painter" and "Making the Most of Your Second Marriage" create instant reader identification.

4.7 *Preparing Your Outline for Submission*

Type up two versions of your outline. The first should list the chapter titles plus all the headings and subheadings you devised. This is the chapter outline. The second is the annotated table of contents, which contains all of the chapter titles, each followed by a descriptive paragraph explaining exactly what you intend to address and accomplish in the chapter.

Publishers like to see both of these. The chapter outline gives them an idea of how your contents page will look to the reader. The annotated table of contents offers a detailed look at your plan for the book.

Part Three

Writing a Self-Help/How-To Proposal

How to Write a Proposal That Sells

5.1   The Sales Pitch for Your Book

Before your self-help/how-to book can reach and help readers, you first have to sell it to a publisher. The *proposal* is the sales pitch for your book. Done right, it will make editors' mouths water.

Don't try to skip this step and just send in a complete manuscript. Publishers buy 90 percent of their books based on proposals. Because the proposal previews your book and details its market, publishers want to read it before reading a complete manuscript. Editors at most big publishing houses are now telling agents that they want to see a fully fleshed-out proposal before looking at a complete nonfiction manuscript.

Even when the author has a complete manuscript, editors usually insist that it be accompanied by a proposal—another good reason to write just one sample chapter first and complete the bulk of the manuscript after you have found a publisher. This makes the proposal as important as your book. Professional writers know this, so they give as much thought and care to their proposals as they do to their books.

This may make proposal writing seem difficult or a lot of work—but it isn't. A good proposal can be written without extraordinary effort and, most importantly, shows that the writer has done his or her homework and is capable of delivering a salable book.

5.2   How Proposals Help You

Even if a publisher doesn't require a proposal, you should create one for your own use. By forcing you to think through crucial aspects of your book before you start writing, a proposal sharpens your understanding of the material and can suggest vital midcourse corrections. Better yet—and this may be a proposal's biggest benefit for a beginning writer—in the process of writing a proposal you'll pick up all the skills you need to write your book.

Proposals can help you in numerous ways:

- Clarify your material.
- Target your market.
- Find the key points that book publishers' sales reps will use to sell your book to stores.
- Encapsulate your book's most important ideas and elements in an exciting, intriguing form.
- Discover weak spots in your organization.
- Put the zing in your work.

5.3   Proposals Save You Time

One reason editors want to see a proposal is that it saves them—and you—wasted effort. About one-half or more of all the manuscripts that publishers receive aren't right for the company. Publishers aren't all the same, and they don't all publish the same kinds of books. Even if it is letter-perfect, your manuscript might not be right for a specific publisher for any number of reasons:

- The publisher doesn't publish books in your subject area.
- The publisher already has a book on the same topic coming out soon.
- Your approach and treatment don't fit the publisher's house style.

An editor might have to wait weeks or even months to find time to read an entire book manuscript—and then plow through a hundred or more pages to determine whether it is the kind of book the firm publishes. What author wants his or her book to sit on a shelf for weeks or months waiting to be read, only to have the editor discover that there was never any chance the publisher could use it?

However, editors say it's easy for them to find the time to review a proposal. They can get to it quickly and can make fast decisions on whether to offer a contract. But if your book isn't appropriate for the imprint, the editor can promptly return your proposal, and you can submit it elsewhere with minimal loss of time. It is not good practice to submit to more than one publisher at a time (called "multiple submissions"), as many publishers will refuse to read your proposal out of hand if they are aware of it.

5.4 Selling Your Book to Publishers—Helping Publishers Sell Your Book

You may not think of your book as a commodity that has to be sold—but it is. You want to sell it to a publisher, don't you? You may think that's an agent's job, but you need to be involved in the selling process as well. Obviously the person most familiar with your book—and in the best position to inform potential publishers about why they should buy it—is you. You know why you wrote it, who it is intended for, and how it will benefit readers. Use your intimate knowledge of the subject matter and audience to help sell your book to publishers. A publisher might know something about the sports world, for example, but you may have access to lists of fan clubs or specialty mail-order catalog firms of which your publisher would not be aware. Informing potential publishers of this could enhance your book's desirability to them and its future sales to readers. Highlight these points in your proposal, and the marketing department can tell exactly why customers would want your book. Your proposal becomes an irresistible sales pitch, first helping you sell your book to a publisher, and then helping them sell it to readers.

Once you've sold your book to a publisher, you want to help them make it a bestseller. Even though they have marketing and promotion departments, they need inside knowledge about your manuscript and its market—knowledge that only you possess.

5.5   What's in a Proposal?

As indicated above, a proposal is both a sales pitch for your book and a marketing plan. When your editor recommends it, every member of the company's "publishing committee" will read your proposal. This includes other editors, important marketing executives, the people in charge of sales, promotion, and publicity, and even the publisher or associate publisher. Each person will mark up the parts of your proposal that relate to his or her sphere of interest.

As a sales document, your proposal literally must have something for everyone—specifically, a section written to satisfy the concerns of every department. It should have the following sections:

- An "Overview" section—a description of what you are selling in a way that makes it sound like a must-have
- A "Comparison" section—an analysis of other books on the subject, comparing them with the unique features of your book that will make it a valuable addition.
- A "Target Audience" section—a description of the intended audience
- A "Marketing" section—an explanation of where and how your book can be sold
- A "Promotion and Publicity" section—a list of all the possible avenues of free promotion and publicity
- An "Estimated Time of Completion" section—the delivery date of your completed manuscript
- Specifications on size and special features—length of manuscript, nontextual information such as charts and illustrations, and so forth

- An "About the Author" page—details on why the author's previous accomplishments guarantee a quality outcome

Altogether, this portion of your proposal should probably run about seven to fifteen double-spaced typewritten pages, depending on how detailed you are. And the more detailed the better when it comes to making your book look like a winner to a publisher.

For a winning sales presentation, you might send along slides, charts, videos, as well as sample chapters and previously published work. You can—and should—do the same with your proposal. Put the finishing touches on your pitch with the following:

- A sample of the product (a sample chapter).
- A description of the product (an annotated table of contents).
- A detailed schema for the book (an outline).
- Material that supports your sales pitch or expertise (enclosures). This material can include newsclips that show the timeliness of your topic, favorable reviews of your previously published work, and a list of your credentials and accomplishments in the field in which you're writing.

It doesn't take much time or effort to put together a proposal, but the payoff can be tremendous: securing a publisher, reaching an audience, and the opportunity to better the lives of people everywhere by sharing your knowledge.

Writing Your Overview

6.1 *Making Your Self-Help/How-To Book Sound Like a Must-Have*

Follow the step-by-step program in this chapter to write the "Overview" section of your proposal. You'll learn how to "hook" editors with your first few words, then keep them reading with skillfully planted attention-grabbers that encapsulate your book's highlights in a few mouth-watering words. Like all the techniques involved in writing self-help/how-to books, creating hooks and attention-grabbers is a skill anyone can learn.

The overview section of your proposal is an editor's first exposure to your book. Pique interest immediately by making your book sound like a must-have. The editor will look forward to learning more about your book with excitement and enthusiasm.

6.1.1 The "Hook"

Publishers are like everyone else. They are excited by the new, the different, the dramatic. Open your proposal with a bold, arresting statement—a hook—that previews the subject or theme of your book, and you'll capture their attention every time.

Consider these classic examples of proposals that came across my desk during my years as an editor. In every case, the hook stopped me dead in my tracks and made me want to read more.

One out of every three girls is sexually abused before she reaches the age of eighteen.

More information has been produced in the last 30 years than in the previous 5,000.

There are six major "flash-points" that cause businesses to fail in their first year.

Each year the number of people in the United States who need exercise increases by two and one half million.

Even experienced golfers who have spent years on the fairways make six critical mistakes.

And a final one:

A special group of people wakes up in the night shaking and soaked with sweat. These are the veterans of the Vietnam War—they are victims of what mental health professionals call Post-Traumatic Stress Syndrome.

You can see the drama, the pain, the implied promise—the hook—in each of these sentences. An opening like one of these is guaranteed to make a publisher feel that the book is one that they will want for their readers. Yet all the authors of these hooks did was find a startling statistic, or a dramatic human situation, and use it to kick off their proposal.

Hopefully, your book is filled with equally dramatic ideas; if so, it's not hard to find them and turn them into a hook.

Developing hooks
1. Take the time to review the research you've done for your book so far. Find a statistic or situation that you think would hook anyone's attention and inspire him or her to read further. You may even find several.
2. Summarize each statistic or situation in one to three dramatic sentences—a paragraph at most.

3. Try out each summary on friends (just like you did with prospective titles and subtitles in Chapter 3).
4. Select what you think is the most effective hook, but save any discards, which you can use when you write the remainder of the overview.
5. Type the word "Overview" at the top of a page. Then type your hook under it.

6.1.2   Attention-Grabbers

Now you're going to apply the same method you used for hooks to create and plant attention-grabbers throughout the rest of your overview. Attention-grabbers are additional statements, as dramatic and compelling as your opening hook, that make your proposal seem so exciting that publishers keep reading to find out what the rest of your book has to offer.

Consider this one, from the proposal for a book on easing the physical and mental strains of pregnancy through dreams: "Seventy percent of pregnant women have dreams filled with negativity and anxiety." Or this one, from the proposal for a book on coping with information overload: "The amount of available information doubles every five years."

Developing attention-grabbers
1. Again, review the research you've done so far. Locate two dozen or more ideas that you feel would arrest someone's attention. Look for material that is
   • New
   • Controversial
   • Dramatic
   • Paradoxical
   • Touching
2. Review any discarded hooks as possible attention-grabbers.
3. Summarize each discarded hook in a dramatic, electrifying sentence (two at most).

4. Try out your attention-grabbers on friends.
5. Put stars by those that get the strongest response, and save them to sprinkle at appropriate points in your overview.

6.2 Writing the Overview

Now that you have an opening hook and some attention-grabbers that you can plant along the way, it's time to actually write the overview.

Let's go back to basics. Remember that your proposal is a sales document. To clinch the sale you want to describe and establish the following:

1. Your potential market—who will want your book
2. Why your market needs the book—the problem it solves or an important void it will fill
3. How your book fulfills readers' needs—the way it addresses the problem or teaches the skill
4. How your book will benefit its readers—ways their lives will be bettered
5. How you can substantiate your claims
6. Your book's special features

6.2.1 Your Potential Market

Once your book has captured a publisher's attention, the first concrete thing your overview should do is explain who your potential readers will be. When publishers feel there is an established market for your book, they feel confident about going ahead with its publication. Publishers want to know the book's intended audience. Who will buy it?

Be creative when you answer this question. Describe your book's readership in the kind of dramatic, arresting way you developed your hook and attention-grabbers. This will keep the publisher's interest going, now that you have captured it.

Describing your reader

1. Think about the audience for your book.
2. Come up with a vivid, exciting way to tell publishers, in a sentence or two, what kind of person—or group—needs your book, who its ideal reader would be. Be creative. Remember, you want to keep a publisher's interest going now that you have captured it.
3. Directly beneath the opening hook, type the description of your reader.

Here's how four successful book proposals pictured their audience: "*The Road to Recovery* is written for the millions who suffer from alcoholism and other forms of substance abuse." Or "Every athlete who seeks an extra 'edge' will want this book." Or "Many people in their mid-forties ask themselves if they have chosen the right career path." Or "Millions of people try to diet every year—yet never lose weight. Why?"

6.2.2 Why Your Market Needs the Book

Second, you need a succinct, compelling statement of why people will need your book. Try to give it flare. Keeping the drama and excitement high is the key to a proposal that sells.

Also, make your description brief. A sentence to a paragraph will do. Let one publisher's suggestions for a self-help/how-to proposal be your guide: "Tell why the book is needed, emphasizing the practical aspects. Come quickly to your major points."

A proposal for a book on adult children of alcoholics made publishers take notice with this touching portrait of the problems its readers faced:

> Few childhoods are more difficult than those in which one or both parents are alcoholic. The emotional damage is often so deep that it carries over into adult life, in the form of troubled relationships with loved ones and coworkers, depression, alcoholism, addiction, compulsive sexuality, child

abuse, and crippling self-doubts. The physical consequences, in the form of stress, heart disease, and psychosomatic illnesses are equally disastrous.

In the next example, the readers' problem was more subtle—but it convinced publishers there was a market for the author's book. "Most people use ten percent or less of their brain power, leaving a vast reserve of mental ability unused." Obviously the need, which was implied, is that we are all leading lives that are less than what they might be if we could tap our unused brainpower.

Here's another compelling explanation of why the author's audience would need her book:

Today men and women increasingly find themselves working side by side as "office couples" in intimate circumstances that can heighten their sexual awareness of each other. If either or both have committed relationships, the results can be devastating. This book offers a new option that shows how the excitement of male/female attraction can be channeled into increased workplace productivity—rather than a destructive affair.

A final example: "Most do-it-yourselfers waste up to one-half of the money they invest in equipment and materials. They could save that money—if they knew a few simple secrets all professional carpenters know."

Describing the problem your book solves
1. Take as long as you need—from an hour to several days—to formulate a succinct, exciting description of the problem or lack your book promises to remedy. Try to capture its urgency and dimension, whether physical, emotional, financial, or all three. Keep the description to a paragraph if you can, but by all means it can be longer if absolutely necessary.

    If it takes you more than one paragraph, try rethinking your approach. This is a sales presentation. You have to get in, grab a publisher's attention, pitch quickly, and get out before the publisher becomes bored. Cut to the chase, as they say in the movies. Give the highlights. Pare your description to the bone if you have to, but hold it to a page and a half at the very longest. You can't risk having an editor become restless before you get to the finish. If your book addresses a cluster of key problems or deficiencies, use a bulleted list (see Chapter 11) to summarize them.

2. Type this description immediately below the description of your reader.

6.2.3 How Your Book Fulfills Readers' Needs

Third, write a paragraph describing how your book will benefit the publisher's audience. Convince a publisher that you have a system that works, and you have taken a major step toward selling your book. Apply the KISSED rule: Keep it short, simple, exciting, dramatic.

The following passage from a winning book proposal makes it easy to see why one author's approach would turn reluctant readers into enthusiastic ones:

> . . . hundreds of easily followed suggestions to spark your child's excitement for the written word; a complete reading program for children of every age; games and activities to involve reluctant and turned-off readers; extensive book and magazine recommendations; suggested record and television entertainment designed to develop reading interest and skills; information about children's book clubs and reading groups.

Another author won her book contract when she told her publisher that her book on power-management would include insights on "middle management, satisfied employees and loyal customers, balancing imagination and hard work, integrating private and business lives, striving to be the best."

Another important rule: If you have been using the approach

described in your book to help people successfully for a number of years, say so in your overview. This kind of information impresses publishers and often clinches the sale. If you have helped hundreds, or even thousands, through personal therapy, seminars, or tapes, let the publisher know. The more successful your system sounds, the more successful your book sounds to publishers. Don't be modest. No one ever sold a product by being modest about its virtues.

Describing the problem your book solves

1. Develop a short, dramatic explanation of how your system works. Be as specific as possible.
2. Immediately following the problem your book solves, explain how your book helps solve that problem. If the explanation is longer than a page, you have overdone it and need to try to compress your description further. The preceding example was only one paragraph, but it was clear and convincing and made the author's approach sound substantial and sensible.

6.2.4 How Your Book Will Benefit Its Readers

Fourth, describe how your book will help readers. Over and over, publishers' guidelines drive this point home. "How does the book benefit those who may buy it?" asks one. "What positive results will they gain?" Another asks, "List the benefits the reader will receive from the information you plan to provide. Be as specific as possible."

Once again, being specific is critical. Every self-help/how-to book aims at making people's lives better. Separate your book from the herd by listing those benefits that are unique to your system or approach. Follow this example from a proposal that instantly garnered its author a contract.

This book spells out proven techniques that help you:

- Get paperwork done in half the time
- Recall facts, dates, and figures

- Do mental calculations at the speed of a computer
- Read a complete book in less time than most people spend on one chapter
- Solve problems that stump others
- Speed-learn any subject

Or emulate this example from a proposal for a book on recovery from relationship dependency. The author promised a book that would help readers learn to

Identify codependence in their lives; let go of their obsession with others; end destructive relationships; nurture and parent themselves; release damaging patterns of the past; recover a sense of completeness; build stronger personal boundaries; make healthier choices; develop healthy intimacy.

When you formulate your book's benefits as cogently as this, publishers will see it as a natural winner.

Describing what your book will do for readers
1. Write a one-page summary (more or less) of what you believe your book will do for readers.
2. Examine this summary carefully. Does it reflect what is unique about your book specifically enough? If not, revise your summary until it does.

6.2.5 How You Can Substantiate Your Claims

Fifth, explain any claim implied in your book's title. Maybe the title contains a word like "miracle," "magic," "big," "complete," "treasury," "rich," "success," or "powerful." Supply one or more examples of how your program is powerful, magical, and so forth. If your title includes a sum of money, detail how that sum can be earned using the principles in your book.

6.2.6 Your Book's Special Features

Sixth, write a final paragraph that stresses any special features your book will have, such as checklists, charts, exercises, quizzes, case histories, or unique and powerful tips—anything and everything special that will make your book more useful to readers.

Your overview is complete. You are already through with the most difficult part of your proposal. The rest is child's play by comparison. You may not realize it, but in the process of writing your overview, you developed about half the skills you need to complete your proposal and write your book.

Making Your Proposal Clinch the Sale

7.1 *Answer Publishers' Questions about Your Book— Before They Ask Them*

The more interested publishers become in your book, the more questions they will have about it. They will want to know who its audience is, how you think it can best be marketed, what experience you've had presenting your ideas to the public, your credentials, and many other matters. You can "clinch the sale" by answering these questions ahead of time in your proposal.

7.2 *Comparing Your Book with the Competition*

Publishers want books that are distinctive and different because readers want books that are distinctive and different. As a sales pitch, your proposal needs a page explaining why your product is superior to the competition. Be specific and honest in your appraisal. To add the clinching argument to your sales presentation, detail what makes your book stand out from others on the same subject.

The comparison you provide helps the editor sell your book to the key people at the publishing firm who make the final decision about acquiring a manuscript. Your comparison also provides the sales department with the kind of ammunition it needs to sell your book to bookstores and chains. These firms are just as reluctant as publishers to give space to a new self-help/how-to–book unless they are convinced it has something unique to offer that other books on the subject lack.

If you are familiar with the other successful books in your field, you can polish off the "Comparison" page in an hour or so. You can't go wrong, according to one leading publisher, as long as you keep your focus on how your book will be better than the competition.

To get you started, here's an actual "Comparison" section from a book on instant learning. Less than a double-spaced page long, it helped clinch the sale of its author's book:

Probably the book's closest competition is Ronald Gross's *Peak Learning* (Tarcher, 1991). Its faults are those of many others on this subject, and what I will say about it is true also of the rest. *Peak Learning* is a good book, but it *takes three chapters before it gets to a single reader exercise. Instant Learning* begins to involve the reader with a "teaser" exercise in the Introduction and *the first full-fledged exercise within the first five pages of the first chapter.*

Peak Learning also devotes a great deal of space to explaining intricate scientific theories about the brain. *Instant Learning* is concerned entirely with application and only minimally with theory. It has just as solid a scientific foundation, but readers won't find this slowing up the text; instead, they can look up my sources in the Bibliography.

Peak Learning also devotes only 150 of its 300 pages directly to helping the reader learn to learn better—the rest is devoted to philosophy and other side issues. All of *Instant Learning* is devoted to developing the learning skills contemporary readers so desperately need.

Now write your own comparison page. Don't hold back on extolling your book's virtues. Convincing publishers it's so special readers will want it, even if they have other books on the subject, is the whole point.

If you don't know what the competition for your book is, find out. The guidelines from one publisher urge, "Go to a library. Go to a bookstore. Check *Books in Print*. [Available at all libraries.]" They also warn first-time authors not to simply state, "There's nothing like my book out there." Instead, they say, "Cite all other key books on that subject area," as proof.

Describing what makes your book unique
1. Type "Comparison" at the top of a page.
2. List a half dozen recent leading titles in your subject area written for the general public. Always include the author, publisher, date of publication, and price.
3. Describe how your book will differ from each of the books in the list: what it does better and what it does that the others don't do at all.

7.3   *Estimating the Size of Your Audience*

Here are a few suggestions for your "Audience" page. Gather figures estimating the size of your book's potential readership. Publishers think in terms of tens and hundreds of thousands, so be careful to list every possibility.

Every self-help/how-to book has not one but several audiences. The key here is to include every possible subsidiary readership that might help contribute to your book's success. These include the following:

• Your primary audience—people who actually have the problem or want the abilities your book concerns.
• A number of subsidiary audiences:
    Relatives, loved ones, and friends of those with an interest in the subject matter.
    Professionals who work in the field.

Others. (I don't know what these might be but, as an expert in your field, you do and can fill in the blanks from here.)

Want a tip that will help you put this part of your sales presentation over in a big way? If you have statistics, use them. If your book is for those who suffer from paralyzing shyness, publishers need to know how many people are affected so they can generate potential sales figures. These figures are important to you, too, because they help publishers determine how much money they should give you as an advance against sales of your book.

If your book is for women and men who appear to have risen as high as they can go in their present jobs or are planning to build an addition to their home—and you can find estimates of the number of people affected—use them by all means. Publishers may know that a particular condition or situation is widespread, but when they read that "more than 4 million adults sit frustrated in dead-end positions unable to advance further in their organizations" or that "over 250,000 American do-it-yourselfers will build an addition to their home this year," publishers sit up and take notice.

If your book concerns problems that carry over into family and professional life, make your proposal even more convincing by estimating the size of those readerships, as well. If your book helps people overcome a problem or provides vitally needed skills, it will contain valuable insights that would be useful to professionals and paraprofessionals. A book on how women can retain self-esteem and a sense of physical attractiveness after a mastectomy might aid physicians in understanding how to ease women through the adjustment to the news of surgery. It will also be of value to psychotherapists, physiotherapists, and others working with women who have had or will soon undergo mastectomies. In addition, there are dozens of support groups in the United States for women who have had mastectomies.

If you offer a new approach to acting, you will appeal to actors, of course, but your book will also be of value to the drama departments of educational institutions as well as private drama schools—

and most public library systems, which are always interested in acquiring important new works on the performing arts.

Spotting, and listing, subsidiary audiences like these is easy, and it establishes that your book can potentially sell tens, perhaps hundreds, of thousands of additional copies—through mail-order and other venues.

Describing the size of your book's audience
1. Type "Audience" at the top of a page.
2. List all the possible readerships.

7.4   *Describing How Your Book Can Be Marketed*

When it comes to the "Marketing" section, share every stray thought you have about where your book might be sold. For most self-help/how-to books, the biggest sale will probably be through regular bookstores. Publishers know this market well, but you can make your book sound like an easy sell and provide publishers with an instant sales pitch by explaining why you think it will appeal to the average bookstore's customers.

Recently, a new potential market, in the form of thousands of specialty bookstores, has sprung up around the country. These bookstores range from establishments specializing in recovery to self-development, women's issues, health, athletics, do-it-yourself activities, the New Age, and beyond. You can get a good feel for the kinds of bookstores serving special markets by looking under "books" in the yellow pages.

A book on how nutrition can reverse psychological conditions (depression, obsessive/compulsive disorder, and others) long considered untreatable should enjoy brisk sales in New Age bookstores, bookstores concentrating on health and healing, and perhaps others. But bookstores wouldn't be this book's only market. It could also be sold through outlets serving those interested in nutrition, fitness, and health, such as health-food stores and specialty catalogs, and organizations like professional associations, peer support groups, and mailing list companies.

How detailed should your "Audience" page be? Let the publishers be your guide. The proposal guidelines from one publisher recommends that authors list any of the following:

- Bookstores
- Specialty stores
- Organizations
- Catalogs
- Publications in which the book could be advertised
    Specialty publications
    Professional publications
    Newsletters
- Other venues that would buy your book, which would depend on the field

Describing how your book can be sold
  1. Type "Marketing" at the top of a page.
  2. In a sentence each, describe every market that comes to mind (for a memory jogger, refer to the preceding list).
  3. Explain why you believe your book would appeal to each market's particular clientele.

7.5 *Showing How Your Book Will Promote Itself*

Use your "Promotion and Publicity" section to alert publishers to every medium and source you know of that might showcase your or your book for free, including magazines, newspapers, television and radio stations, the Internet, and other electronic media. There are literally thousands of sources eager to offer you time and exposure gratis.

Newspapers must fill up hundreds of columns with fresh material every day. Magazine editors are constantly searching for new ideas they can use to spark articles for next month's issue. Television and radio stations must always find new guests to interview. If you have a book that will be of benefit to a significant portion of their audience, one with something new and fresh to say, most of these sources will be eager to interview you or quote from your book.

Let's face it. Quality aside, what really makes any book a bestseller is publicity—and plenty of it. Today, there are more publicity outlets for self-help and how-to books than ever before. By creating a "Promotion and Publicity" section that shows publishers the special promotional opportunities for your book, you prove your book's bestseller potential. After all you have learned so far, this will be a snap.

7.5.1 Talk Shows

Publishers look for books that have talk-show appeal. Ten minutes on a national television talk show sells more copies than ten full-page ads in *The New York Times* or *People* magazine. So can an hour on radio. If you feel your book will have talk-show potential with the electronic media, tell publishers that in your proposal—and explain why.

Talk shows need new guests and new topics with a unique enough message to keep their audiences tuning in every day. Most have teams of producers whose job is to keep a constant search for self-help/how-to authors like you with fresh topics or fresh slants on old topics. If your book offers assistance or instruction on a subject that affects a large section of their audience, most talk shows will welcome you with open arms.

If your theme touches the lives of millions, telling publishers this is a good start. But, remember, they and you are competing for talk-show time against hundreds of other authors. You can add to your book's potential value to talk-show hosts by looking for and describing the dramatic and theatrical possibilities for your book.

For example, you might be able to bring on a group of people to tell their own inspiring stories and how you helped them. Or you might be able to demonstrate how to revitalize old T-shirts by tie-dyeing them live on stage. Or if your approach is controversial, and there are people who have openly challenged it, they might be willing to debate the issues with you on talk shows—creating the kind of dramatic fireworks that audiences, producers, and hosts can't resist.

7.5.2 Newspaper and Magazine Articles

Publishing professionals call newspapers and magazines print media. They constitute the single biggest bonanza of potential publicity available to authors and publishers. They offer two potential sources of publicity: interviews and feature articles. As for interviews that center on you personally, readers and editors like these because they have a personal touch. Feature articles cover the entire subject area of your book and quote extensively from you and the book. The advantage of features is that everyone who is interested in your subject is likely to read them. Publishers know about many of these publications but won't always know why your book will be of specific appeal to them. You convince publishers that your book will promote itself when you take the time to explain why your book will interest various publications and types of publications.

Magazines. Thousands of national magazines, on every level, from newsstand publications such as *Time*, *Fortune*, *Cosmopolitan*, and *Reader's Digest* to specialty publications such as *Health and Fitness* and *Recovery*—and even professional journals and business and trade journals—are actively looking for professionals with new self-help/how-to books they can cover. The same is true of the hundreds of regional magazines published in cities and states across the country. Almost every national magazine has its local analog. Always list all the magazines that your book might appeal to and why you think their readership would be interested in it.

Newspapers.   Because they come out daily, newspapers are even more anxious to find someone with a book like yours. Helping readers to improve their lives and abilities is part of a newspaper's mission. Every locality has numerous newspapers, large and small. The Los Angeles area, for instance, has two major daily newspapers, more than a dozen community dailies, and more than one hundred weekly, or three-times weekly, smaller community papers. Each one is seeking writers from their community, or visiting their community, whom they can introduce to their readers. List local papers that will be interested in covering your book because you are a hometown success story, and explain why your book might be of interest to national papers.

7.5.3   Reviews

Most magazines and newspapers have book review sections, and the self-help/how-to book is among the most widely reviewed. Reviews are another source of free publicity. Enough good reviews can make a book a bestseller. If there are publications large or small, national or local, that you are certain would be eager to review your book, make sure you enumerate them on your "Promotion" section.

7.5.4   The World Wide Web, E-Mail, and Electronic Bulletin Boards

In the last few years, a host of electronic methods of disseminating information has sprung into existence. If you have a modem and can access the World Wide Web, e-mail, or electronic bulletin boards, you can search out those devoted to areas of interest that overlap the subject area of your book, for example, a bulletin board for parents of children with Down syndrome, or practitioners of the martial arts, or Alcoholics Anonymous members, or women actively seeking to network together to enhance their careers. By uploading teasers for your book—benefits, portions of the text, or announcements of its forthcoming publication—you can bypass publishers, bookstores, and the media, and pitch your work straight to its readership. A number of recent bestsellers started this way.

7.5.5 Your Own Media Experience

If you have had media experience—appeared on talk shows, given newspaper interviews, lectured or otherwise spoken before microphones or the public—tell publishers this in your proposal. Authors who can articulate their ideas well in front of others are easy to promote. Knowing you can do this fuels a publisher's enthusiasm for your book.

Detailing how your book should be promoted
1. Type "Promotion and Publicity" at the top of a page.
2. List every source that might present a promotional opportunity for your book.

7.6 Estimating Length, Format, and Time of Completion

There are a few other questions publishers have when they are interested in your book. The answers help them make important decisions about format, pricing, and unit costs—even how much they should pay you for your book.

7.6.1 Describing Front Matter

Front matter is the written material in your book that precedes the first chapter. Not all the following will apply to your book, but front matter can include the following:

- Title page
- Copyright page
- Dedication

- Table of contents
- List of illustrative materials
- Foreword
- Preface
- Acknowledgments
- Introduction

If you plan to include any of these sections, complete the following steps:

1. Type the heading "Front Matter."
2. List each item you plan to include, giving a rough estimate of its length.

7.6.2 Describing Back Matter

Back matter is the written material in your book that follows the last chapter. Not all the following will apply to your book, but back matter can include the following:

- Appendixes
   Chronology
   Recommended reading
   Resources
- Glossary
- References if necessary
- Bibliography
- Index

If you plan to include any of these sections, complete the following steps:

1. Type the heading "Back Matter."
2. List each item you plan to include, giving a rough estimate of its length.

7.6.3 Describing Illustrative Material

If drawings, charts, or forms will benefit your book, give publishers an approximate idea of your plans now. Take the time to explain why illustrative material will enhance the reader's understanding of your book. Then give an estimate of the total number of illustrations to be used. Publishers prefer that you estimate in multiples of ten. They admit that this is hard to do so early in the process but add that your estimate gives an approximation of what you plan to do. Illustrative material includes the following:

- Black and white drawings
- Photographs
- Charts
- Tables
- Graphs
- Blank forms

As I was writing this chapter, a publisher called and asked me to work with a self-help author whose book had "more charts and graphs than you could shake a stick at." The publisher's concluding words: "Nobody wants that highly theoretical stuff."

Inform publishers of how much, if any, illustrative material your book will have. This allows them to estimate the potential production cost and what they will have to charge readers. Every single illustration or graph that is added to a book raises its publication cost. If the amount of illustrative material you plan to include will raise the final price tag higher than most readers are willing to pay, the publisher can begin working with you now to determine which pieces are the most vital and which you might be able to do without.

Knowing about the illustrative material you plan to include also helps publishers begin thinking about the best size and format for your book. If your book has photographs whose details need to be clearly seen, the publisher might decide to print them all on glossy paper. (The use of glossy paper drives up costs, so this leads to pricing considerations.)

But beware: When it comes to charts, graphs, and tables—don't overdo it. While they can help make your points clearer, they can also turn off many readers by making your book look too technical. One publisher cautions prospective authors who are considering adding illustrative matter to their books to "limit them to the extent they make a necessary, potentially profitable contribution to the book."

Describing illustrative material
1. Type the heading "Illustrative Material."
2. In a paragraph, describe what you intend to use as illustrative material and how it will add to readers' understanding of your book.

7.6.5 Estimating Length

Give the publisher some idea of how long your finished manuscript will be in double-spaced pages. This allows the publisher to estimate the length of the published book, which in turn gives some idea of what to charge for the book in order to realize a profit. One sentence is generally enough. (Be sure to include front and back matter and illustrative material in your estimate.) A good rule of thumb is that 250 words equals one double-spaced manuscript page. An example is, "The author estimates the finished manuscript will be approximately 85,000 words or 375 manuscript pages."

Remember, you are only giving an estimate in your proposal. It's not written in stone, and your final draft doesn't have to be exactly that length. Publishers allow for this because they assume that your final draft will be a *little* longer or shorter than your estimate.

How much of a fudge factor do you have? I called six editor friends and asked them how much longer or shorter a writer's book had to be than the estimate to really give their publishing company trouble. Most agreed that 25 percent was the demarcation line. They requested their authors to immediately notify them when a book's length began to deviate 25 percent or more away from the original estimate. Most editors will ask you to cut your manuscript if it is more than 25 percent over the estimate. If you object to any cutting, you'll need to discuss it with your editor—so it is best to contact your editor as soon as it becomes apparent that your manuscript is going to run significantly over—or under. Depending on the title and the situation, it might be desirable to have a longer (or shorter) book—but your publisher still needs as much notice as possible to allow time to make necessary adjustments in catalog copy, cost estimates, and retail price, and notify booksellers who may have already placed advanced orders based on the old price.

There's another advantage to estimating how long your book will be. It helps publishers determine whether your book is too long for its market (i.e., will cost more than most readers of this type of book have proven willing to pay in the past). If so, the publisher may suggest trimming or (rarely) expanding your book. That way you can plan for the altered word length before you begin writing, rather than discovering your manuscript is too long at the last minute and having to trim 50 or 100 pages, or more.

One prospective author who attended my classes on how to write bestsellers recently submitted a proposal for a vast biographical encyclopedia of women soldiers, police officers, federal agents, and spies. The publisher who accepted it suggested she tighten her book's theme and limit it to women involved in warfare: soldiers, freedom fighters, guerrilla warriors, and spies. The publisher wanted her to hold her material on women who served as peace officers, state troopers, treasury agents, and others for a later book.

Describing your book's length
1. Type the heading "Estimated Length of Manuscript."
2. Give the estimated length either in words or in double-spaced manuscript pages (include all front and back matter).

7.6.6 Estimating Time of Completion

Publishers need to know how long you believe it will take you to finish the first draft of your book. This enables them to tentatively

77

schedule the year and season of your book's release. If you finish your manuscript ahead of time or a few weeks late, there's no problem. But if you are going to be a month or so late, be sure to let your editor know as far in advance as you can. This will allow the publisher to reschedule a delivery date with a minimum of disruption.

Describing how long your book will take to write
1. Type the heading "Estimated Time of Completion."
2. Considering all you know about other demands on your time, and your own writing speed, give your best guess about how long it will take you to write the entire book—for example, "Ideally I believe it would take me eighteen (18) months to complete this book, but I could deliver the manuscript faster if the publishing schedule required it."

7.7 About the Author—Establishing Your Credentials

Establishing your credentials is a very important part of your proposal. Although it is only a page long, experienced authors think carefully about what goes into the biography they send to publishers. The goal is to write a one-page summary of your personal and professional experience that makes your qualifications for writing your book crystal clear. Publishers want to know that their authors have solid backgrounds that will command the attention of readers, reviewers, and the media.

If you are someone who is collaborating with an expert, you will want to write an "About the Author" page that makes your expert seem like the only logical choice for writing such a book. And if your own name will appear on the cover, or the publisher is aware there is a collaborator, you will want to do the same in regard to your own qualifications and expertise as a writer.

Don't fall down here and give in to an acute case of modesty. We were all taught not to blow our own horn, but right now it's vital you do so. You are selling a product—yourself. You have to pitch yourself with the same enthusiasm you would a friend or a relative.

The goal is to establish yourself as someone uniquely qualified to write your book. Cite relevant degrees, affiliations, awards, job experience, books, articles, any media exposure, and anything else you can think of.

As writing gurus Barbara Toohey and June Nierman write, "This is no time for modesty. Pull out every credential you have and wham the publisher over the head with it."

Self-help book publisher Jeremy Tarcher points out that all his bestselling books came from authors with solid experience.

> The most successful books my company has published—Betty Edwards' *Drawing on the Right Side of the Brain*, of which we sold over 1.5 million copies, or Gabriele Rico's *Writing the Natural Way*—are based on the author's deep experiences of that material. They have tried it out again and again until it represents a working system.

Another publisher's proposal guidelines give the same advice for writing your "About the Author" page:

> Put greatest stress on positions you hold or have held or experience you have had, that qualify you to write about your subject. If you are writing on intimacy skills, for example, mention your experience working successfully with those who lack such skills in situations like private counseling, clinics and group therapy workshops. Mention other experiences only when they relate directly to your subject.

If you have won awards for your quilts, or taken prizes in high-diving, and this is the subject of your book—be sure to make this clear.

Unless directly relevant, hobbies, experience in wholly unrelated areas, and personal matters are best omitted. As one publisher warns, "Keep your focus on the subject at hand; do not mention irrelevancies or family history. The main point here is: What background, training and experience gives you the authority to write this book."

Approximately half of your "About the Author" page should be devoted to summarizing any academic and professional qualifications you have. The second half should be devoted to the experiences that have led to your expertise in this area. (If you are a ghostwriter, detail your collaborator's credentials.) Try to keep your tone lively and interesting. The goal is to make publishers realize that you are an author whose book they must have on their list.

Describing yourself
1. At the top of a page, type "About the Author."
2. Discuss your background and how it qualifies you to write your book.

7.8   Enclosures—Sales Enhancers

Boost your proposal's effectiveness with the strategic use of *enclosures*. There are several types of enclosures. Include as many as you can find.

7.8.1   Endorsements

Books sell better when their covers are filled with quotes from experts or other successful authors recommending the book to readers. Most likely you know at least a few such people yourself—especially because you are deeply involved enough in a field to be able to write a self-help/how-to book. Adding a page listing the names of a few potential endorsers will make your book all that more attractive to publishing committees.

7.8.2   Questions Your Book Answers and Benefits It Will Bestow

Talk-show hosts, bookstore owners, and reviewers will want to know about important questions your book answers. If you are writing a book about how women can empower themselves careerwise in the workplace, it would probably answer questions such as these:

- What are the biggest obstacles facing women seeking careers in the workplace today?
- How widespread are these problems?
- How do these obstacles affect women's self-esteem?
- How can women overcome those obstacles?
- How can women work together to achieve their individual career goals?

Enclose a dozen or so exciting questions such as these on a separate page headed "Questions This Book Answers."

7.8.3   Benefits

You have already listed the benefits readers will get from your book in the overview, but this is one of the key elements in selling publishers and readers your book, so you can't overemphasize this aspect of your work. Provide an expanded list of benefits on a separate page or two. Title it "Benefits of Reading This Book."

7.8.4   Visual Aids

Show and tell is part of any effective sales presentation. Lend your proposal compelling visual impact with photocopies of news articles related to your book or material that shows you are a recognized expert.

7.8.5   The Visual Aids Enclosure Checklist

The following checklist will keep you from overlooking anything that might make an impressive, attention-getting visual aid.

☐   Illustrative material from newspapers and magazines that shows a great need for your book and a large audience that will buy it.

☐   Notices and programs for professional speaking engagements or workshops and seminars you have attended.

☐   Newspaper and magazine articles about or quoting you.

☐   Tapes of any radio or television show appearances, or copies of correspondence with producers and hosts.

When you've assembled the inclusions, your sales presentation is almost complete. What publishers need next is an idea of what form the book will take. You can show them this with a sample chapter.

Part Four

Writing the Sample Chapter

8

Chapter Writing Step by Step

8.1 Picking Your Sample Chapter

Keep these two rules in mind when choosing which sample chapter to write and include in your proposal:

1. It should be representative and showcase your ideas in action.
2. It should be easy to write.

Now, here's how to go about writing it.

8.2 The ABCs of Chapter Writing

Formulating a self-help/how-to chapter is based on the same principles of sound journalism you learned in school: First, tell them what you are going to tell them; then tell them; then tell them what you told them.

This is another variant of the old rule of three: What I tell you three times is true. In other words, ideas you reinforce three times in the space of a chapter are likely to be remembered.

I call this the ABC system for writing chapters:

- A stands for the introduction, where you tell readers what your chapter will be About.

- *B* is for the Body of your chapter, where you develop your theme in all its aspects.
- C stands for the Conclusion, where you sum up the implications of what you've said.

When you begin thinking of writing a chapter, think "About, Body, Conclusion"—it will keep you focused on the three critical building blocks of good chapters. But it will do more than that.

These three letters are really the formula for writing each and every section and subsection of your book. Introduce the main topic of the section, develop it, and bring it to a conclusion. Even apply it to paragraphs. Kick each off with an interesting topic sentence and then amplify it in the body of your paragraph.

Finalizing the outline
1. Review the chapter's outline one last time. Have you allowed for an opening that states the chapter's central theme? Does the body develop a series of clearly defined points? Does it contain a culminating skill or insight?
2. Revise the outline, if necessary.

Slip another sheet of paper into the typewriter (or open a new computer file). You're about to start with A and zip right through your sample chapter.

8.3   A—*Encapsulating What It's about in a Hook*

To get readers excited about reading a chapter, you have to reach out and grab them. This may sound like a tough assignment, but it's a skill learned while devising the opening hook for your proposal (Chapter 6).

Creating hooks is another fun part of writing your book. It's challenging. It offers you a chance to stretch your mental muscles. It breaks up the pace of writing.

Let's apply your skill at devising dramatic statements to your chapter. Before you write it—and every time you prepare to write any chapter—take a few moments to develop a strong, opening hook, one so dramatic or so touching or so puzzling that it immediately snares the readers' interest and carries them several pages on sheer momentum alone.

As easy as the fine art of creating hooks is, it's about to get easier. You're going to learn a bit of insider knowledge that will simplify the whole process of developing your hooks. There are only three kinds of hooks. Once you know them, you have three ready-made templates you can use to turn out the opening hooks to order. The three main types of hooks are as follows:

1. Have you ever?
2. The case history
3. The provocative, dramatic statement

Some self-help/how-to authors use the same kind of hook at the openings of all their chapters. They like the uniformity. Other writers like to vary the kind of hooks they use. They feel this keeps readers interested. This is another of those areas where you must use your own judgment and decide which approach is more to your particular tastes or needs.

8.3.1   Hook 1: Have You Ever?

Ask the question "Have you ever?" at the start of a chapter. Follow it with a list of common experiences that people with the problem you discuss or who lack the skill you teach are likely to have experienced. This hooks readers, because you are describing personal experiences into which they never dreamed anyone had insight. They have to keep reading to discover how much more about their personal situation you might know.

"Have you ever?" can be the ideal hook for your first chapter—and a sure attention-getter at the opening of any chapter. If your sample chapter focuses on pointing the way to financial success, a dramatic opening hook might be "Have you ever . . .

- felt your daydreams of millions were only idle fancies?"
- feen an opportunity you let slip by earn profits for others?"
- decided the amount of money you really want is beyond your ability to earn?"
- believed you could never be a multimillionaire because people who become multimillionaires have some special ability that ordinary people like you don't possess?"

At this point, most people are probably able to answer yes to every one of these questions. They are hanging on to the author's words. They identify with everything the author is saying and half-expect to be told they are wrong—that earning millions is possible for them. They will continue to read in order to find out why and how the author thinks they can achieve financial success.

8.3.2   Hook 2: The Case History

Case histories (also called anecdotes) hook readers because they are miniature soap operas. All humans have a need to compare themselves to others; it helps us maintain our sense of balance as individuals. That's one reason why both men and women love gossip—though they sometimes gossip about different kinds of things. We just can't resist the inside story of someone else's private sufferings or triumphs.

Case histories also hook readers because the people in them face the same situations your readers do. Discovering that others have endured the same troubles gives most readers a sense of reassurance. They also have to know whether the life story of someone so much like themselves turned out positive or negative. (You will discover in-depth tips on constructing and troubleshooting case histories in Chapter 12.)

8.3.3 Hook 3: The Provocative, Dramatic Statement

You've already learned about the value of hook 3 while creating a dramatic opening statement for the overview to your proposal. You also developed the knack for creating such a hook. Framing your chapter's central theme in a vivid, intriguing sentence (or sentences) is an infallible method of capturing the reader's attention every time. It makes the reader want to see what follows, makes him or her hope that it will be equally dramatic.

Professionals know that opinions and statements can be made bold and startling in dozens of ways. You could use the following:

- A paradox—"People who genuinely love one another often have frequent fights."
- A startling statistic—"Last year 200 American women became millionaires—you could have been one of them."
- A provocative question—"What is the one thing no winning athlete ever tells another?"
- Proactive—"You can build furniture that looks better than store-bought—and at half the price."
- Human drama—"Anger, anxiety, hot flashes, sudden extremes of hypersexuality and total lack of response. We are talking about men like you who have entered the almost unsuspected male change-of-life—male menopause."

With all these suggestions, you've probably already begun to develop the habit of thinking in hooks and have gotten an inspiration for one that will kick off your sample chapter with a bang. Later, after your book is sold, you will need hooks for every chapter of your book. If keeping readers reading is your goal, try developing hooks for the major sections and subsections of your chapters as well.

Writing your hook
1. Type the number and name of the chapter at the top of a page. Skip a few lines.

2. Find a way to write a dramatic encapsulation of the chapter's theme.
3. Write it down.

8.4   B—*Writing the Body, One Heading at a Time*

Tackle your chapter one heading at a time. It takes no more effort to lift a brick than it does to dash off a page.

The truth is, best-sellers are built—not born. And, like everything else, they are built one brick at a time. You will build your chapters the same way—only you'll be doing it heading by heading.

You already developed the topic headings for your chapters in the outline that accompanies your proposal (Chapter 4). All you have to do now is write a paragraph or two under each heading expanding on the point you want to make.

When you add all those paragraphs together, you will have completed your chapter. And at the same time, you will have acquired all the skills you need to write the remainder of the chapters in your book.

Writing a chapter
1. Under your hook, type the first heading for that chapter from your final chapter outline.
2. Set down, exactly as you would explain it to a friend, whatever you want to say under that heading.
3. Go on to the next heading or subheading, and continue until you reach the end of the chapter.

8.5   C—*Bringing Your Chapter to a Conclusion*

The goal of a successful conclusion is to help readers understand its impact and what you accomplished. Give them a sense of what you originally hoped the chapter would do for them. Let them know they have just read something important and why.

Conclude your chapter with a few paragraphs detailing one or more of the following:

- A review of the chapter's elements
- The theme's connection to the reader's life
- Details on how the chapter helped
- A discussion of the chapter's larger implications
- An explanation of how the chapter leads to the following one

Writing a conclusion
1. Type out a concluding paragraph doing one or more of the above.
2. Review it and ask yourself whether what you have written leaves a heightened sense of the chapter's significance.

8.6   How Long Is a Chapter?

At this point, you may be wondering, What with openings and closings and developing points and all—just exactly how long is a chapter anyway? This is a question that puzzles all beginners, and it's not hard to see why.

The real answer is, however long a chapter has to be to fully present and develop your ideas. Practically speaking, fifty double-spaced pages is too long. In my experience as an editor, most chapters turned out to be twenty to thirty manuscript pages when completed.

Longish chapters are a sign you may have too much material for a single chapter and should look at it with an eye to breaking it up into two or more parts. Extremely short chapters might suggest that you really have hold of a subtheme that belongs within a chapter, not a theme that can carry a chapter on its own. But there have been two-page chapters that worked and sixty-page chapters that worked. The bottom line is that when you find yourself with material that doesn't fit logically or thematically with anything else, make it a chapter, no matter what its length. Again, let your own judgment of what's right for your book be your guide.

8.7   *Beyond the Sample Chapter*

As noted in Chapter 2, it's best to write only your sample chapter initially and then wait until your book has sold to start on the rest. This saves you from having to scrap work if a publisher wants your book but requests changes in the organization or content as indicated in your chapter outline (see Chapter 4).

It's not necessary to write the chapters in order. When you are ready to start on the remaining chapters in your book, most professionals recommend beginning with those you believe will be the easiest to write. This helps you further develop your chapter-writing skills so you will be fully prepared when the time comes to tackle more difficult passages.

Style Made Easy

9.1 Five Keys to a Winning Style

Style is the way you put words together to get your particular message across the way you want it received. Doesn't sound too difficult does it? You are using style every time you talk to someone, particularly when you choose words to achieve a goal or establish a mood.

Want to develop a people-pleasing style? Write what you have to say the way you would talk to someone about it (even address them as "you"). Most people think of style as complicated, intellectual, or "arty," but that isn't what style is about. Style isn't correct grammar, either. Publishers have editors and copyeditors to help you with that.

Have you ever noticed that what you say and how you say it sound different when you are angry? When you are being humorous? When you are sad? When you talk to parents, employers, or a lover?

The fact is you are already the master of many different styles. One of them is the style that makes self-help/how-to books reader favorites. Professionals call it the *conversational style*. In addition, following four more simple literary tricks will have you writing in a winning style. If you steer your course by sticking to the list below while you write, you will draw people in and keep them reading. Together, they are the five keys to people-pleasing prose:

1. Write person to person—conversational style.
2. Write in a warm, supportive style.
3. Write the reader into your book.
4. Write simply and clearly.
5. Write using nonsexist language.

9.2 *Writing Person to Person—Conversational Style*

Writing conversationally just means writing in the same kind of language you would use if you were talking to someone. Keep whatever you have to say to everyday terms. (All trade "secrets" seem obvious when they are explained.) I call this "writing person to person," but many writers and editors call it conversational style. Either way, the principle is the same.

Imagine you are at a party. You meet an intelligent person interested in the subject of your book. He or she asks you to go into detail. Now, write your book in exactly the same words you would use to describe it to that person.

Write about people in the same words and phrases that they typically use to think about themselves. For example, most of us tend to think in terms of "people" and "men and women," not in clinical terms such as "human beings" and "individuals." We think about how we "act" in a situation, not how we "behave." We tend to think of ourselves as "having problems," not "suffering from syndromes." Stick to informal, more personal phrases like these, and readers will sense that you are a comfortable presence they can trust.

Avoid stodgy words and phrases such as "rationale," "methodology," and "theoretically." You say the same thing and keep it interesting when you remember to translate into everyday terms such as "guidelines for," "blueprint for," and "what to do when."

Say things to the reader like, "When you communicate well, you promote your own best interests." Don't use turnoffs like, "People who don't know how to communicate well are at a loss." The first example connects the information to readers' lives; the second is abstract and impersonal.

Looking at your writing this way is particularly helpful if you have been trained to do much academic or professional work. It's natural to fall into the patterns in which we have been trained, unless we have a different model to go by. By writing for an imaginary listener, you phrase things in a way anybody can understand.

9.3   A Warm, Supportive Style

People with a serious personal crisis or those set on acquiring new abilities often worry that they are not good learners—or that change and growth are beyond them. They need a warm, comforting arm around their shoulders. They want reassurance, a sense of hope, and the knowledge that you understand and sympathize with their plight.

You can tell them this—and you should. But you can also make them feel it by writing in a warm, personal, supportive style. Follow these two simple rules:

- Be nonjudgmental—avoid language that stigmatizes.
- Be reassuring and optimistic.

9.3.1   Be Nonjudgmental (Avoid Language That Stigmatizes)

Show readers that you are on their side. People who search out self-help/how-to books often feel negative about themselves and their ability to acquire skills. Concentrate on the positive and downplay the negative; in this way, you leave readers with positive, healthy feelings about themselves.

Most people are overly critical of themselves. They cringe when someone tells them they have done something "wrong" or made "bad" choices. Win readers' confidence by making it clear that you know they have always done the best they can. Emphasize what the reader can do "right" and "better choices" the reader could make.

If you are a professional, call those you have helped "clients," not "patients." Never use words that could be considered pejorative or stigmatizing. "Client" suggests a healthy relationship between equals, whereas "patient" suggests someone dependent with an illness.

9.3.2   Be Reassuring and Optimistic

Give readers frequent reassurance that they can learn a technique or overcome a problem. It is not enough to just tell readers *what* to do. Inform them that "others just like them" have successfully used your program or learned just the skill you are teaching, or emphasize how easy your program is to learn.

Most people have negative images of themselves as learners. Others are afraid that the instructions in books will be difficult or hard to follow. Others are frightened, worried, or in pain. Some are victims of self-defeating behaviors that they are certain they cannot change.

Some readers will have more trouble picking up your ideas than others. Acknowledge that. Reassure them that, although they might have difficulty or fail—at first—it will all come together if they keep trying. Point out that everyone who follows your program eventually succeeds.

9.4   *Writing the Reader into Your Book*

Give your book a personable touch by talking to the reader directly—the way I have talked to you throughout this book. Simply address them as "you." Everyone is the center of his or her own universe. Readers with problems or in search of needed skills are focused on themselves. They are not interested in reading about "patients" or "clients" or "others"; they are interested in reading about themselves.

Use the word "you" as often as possible, along with phrases such as "people like you," "your childhood," and "your goal." This also means minimizing terms such as "ACAs," "addicts," and "their difficulties."

Of course, sometimes "you" isn't appropriate, and talking in terms of "others" or "people" or "women and men" or even "us" and "we" is a necessity. But if you keep in mind that you want to speak directly to your readers by addressing them as "you," you will have mastered the knack of bestseller writing.

Does writing like this really make that much of a difference? Just ask yourself this: Have you ever been someplace where there were several people and suddenly someone yelled, "Hey, you!" Did you turn and look, just to be sure, even though you were sure the call wasn't meant for you? If so, then you know the power of addressing "you."

Ready for a pop quiz? What's wrong with this sentence: "Fear is debilitating." That's right. There's no person in it—the sentence lacks a subject.

Now, take out a piece of paper, write the person back into this sentence. If you wrote something like "Fear can debilitate you" or "Fear can be debilitating for everyone," congratulate yourself. You have just developed the ability to personalize your sentences and add enormous warmth to your book. (I told you this was easy.)

9.5   Style—Keep It Simple

The more simply and plainly you write, the better. Ernest Hemingway, considered one of the great stylists of the American language, is celebrated for his short, crisp, declarative sentences. When it comes to writing, simplicity equals clarity.

Simplicity means you reach all the people you want to help with your book. Surveys show that most men and women have difficulty understanding sentences longer than twelve words. The more successful you are at keeping it simple, the better your chances of reaching the vast audience that makes a book a bestseller.

Keeping your writing simple also means minimizing dependence on technical or clinical jargon that makes your book seem difficult. Of course, everyone has to use technical wording sometimes—in writing about post-traumatic stress syndrome, for instance. But always define a technical term in everyday language the first time you use it. This may sound like a tall order at first, but you will get the hang of it just by reading the following examples.

Skip academic phraseology such as "implies a pattern of associated distress or disability in one or more areas" or "the diagnostic hierarchy accords the primacy of diagnosis to the major debilitating mental disorder." Say the same thing in everyday language. The first example, in everyday language, merely means, "A client's main problem has caused a pattern of other problems."

Ready for another pop quiz? I want you to put down this book and take a while to translate the second example, the "diagnostic hierarchy" sentence, into conversational English. Take two or three different stabs at it, if you like, and then come back.

Do you have your attempts? Fine. If the author was writing outside your field, and you had difficulty understanding what he was saying, then you can imagine how the reader feels when reading something written in the technical jargon of your field.

So, what's the right answer? How should those pesky lines be rewritten? There is no single answer. Any approach that puts the ideas into words the average person might understand is fine. (You will find my own version at the end of this chapter.)

9.6   *Developing Nonsexist Language*

Here's one rule you should never break: Eschew language that might be construed as sexist. Choose phrases that don't exclude members of either sex. Successful authors don't exclude—they include. After all, you want everyone who could benefit from it, whatever their gender, to read your book.

The way we use the English language is always changing. We no longer use many words and phrases that were common in the early

1900s, and in their place new terms and terminologies have evolved. Did you know the rule against split infinitives only dates from the 1930s?

Once, writers (female and male) used "he" to represent any general person whose gender wasn't specified, or who could have been either male or female—for example, "If a client wants to turn an ailing corporation around, he always has the option of 'going back to basics.'" Today that's changed. Just as a man might feel uncomfortable at reading a book whose examples are all about "her" and "she," so a woman might feel the same way about one whose examples are mostly about "he" and "his."

Unfortunately, in English, all the singular pronouns for people are gender-based: "he" and "she." The only neutral pronouns are plural: "they" and "them." This can make gender-balancing your book and freeing it from gender bias a bit awkward.

At the moment, there is no single solution, and most of the current approaches are clumsy at best. One approach to this problem is to use "he or she" or "women and men" (and keep varying which gender goes first). Another is to simply address "he" and "she" in alternate chapters (as is commonly done in modern parenting books). When in doubt, use "person."

Of course, sometimes, as when you are writing a book exclusively for men or women, it is appropriate to use only "he" or "she." But when that happens, it is best to state in your introduction that you will be doing so.

[Answer to how I rewrote the "diagnostic hierarchy" bit: "Psychotherapists concentrate on diagnosing and treating a client's most severe problem first."]

10

Headings and Subheadings

10.1 Using Headings and Subheadings to Keep the Reader Reading and Highlight Key Ideas

Use headings and subheadings to sum up the key point or subject matter of the material in a section or subsection. Put a heading or subheading before each key change of subject. Calling attention to important ideas like this helps reinforce them in the reader's memory.

Headings provide readers with a powerful visual reference tool. Simply by glancing through your headings, readers can quickly and effortlessly locate a section they want to review. Notice how easy it is to find "Five Shortcuts to Great Headings" in this chapter, for example.

Let's say that the most important idea in a section (or subsection) is that visualizing a quiet, tranquil ocean can reduce anxiety before public speaking. Precede that material with a heading in bold type that says "A Cure for Stage Fright." Or you might be writing about drying plaster of paris quickly in a microwave oven. Precede this material with a heading like "Flash-Drying Plaster of Paris."

Go a step further. Lure readers from one idea or element to the next by capturing their excitement with an inviting, humorous, or dramatic heading. When people see a clever heading, it makes them want to read what's under it.

As a self-help/how-to author, what you have to offer is more than useful: it is stimulating ideas and techniques. Readers can't know that unless you communicate that excitement to them. A good heading leaves people eagerly looking forward to what you have to say next.

A great heading does the following:

- Describes the content of the section it heads.
- Arouses curiosity.
- Is intriguing and dramatic.
- Makes a bold promise.
- Has snap or sizzle.

The headings that follow captured my attention the first time I read them. They may spark ideas of your own.

Successful Men and Women Are Not Smarter Than You

"Incestuous" Friendships

Why Most Companies Miss Up to Half Their Market

The Science of Eating For Success

The Selective Attention Trap

Pseudoidentity

Improve Athletic Performance by 25 Percent with One Simple Trick

How To Eat All the Dessert You Want—and Still Lose Weight

Double Your Income in One Year

You Can Avoid the Risk of Heart Attack and Stroke

The "Batman Complex"

Create headings as exciting as the material they summarize, and they become an irresistible lure that draws readers and keeps them reading. It only takes a few minutes to generate great headings. The time spent developing just the right heading is never wasted. The insider shortcuts in this chapter will help get you jump-started.

10.2 Five Shortcuts to Great Headings

You've already got all the skills you need for creating headings with sizzle. You picked them up while finalizing your book and chapter titles (Chapters 3 and 4). It's easy to apply them to devising headings and subheadings. Here are five powerful shortcuts that show you how to do exactly that:

1. Phrase headings in everyday language.
2. Create headings that are lively and intriguing.
3. Coin a new word or phrase.
4. Make a bold promise.
5. Keep headings upbeat.

10.2.1 Phrase Headings in Everyday Language

Everyone understands what you mean by "Thinking about Thinking"; few would understand "Metacognition," although both mean exactly the same thing. Academic and technical terms only turn readers off, particularly those in search of help or know-how.

10.2.2 Create Headings That Are Lively and Intriguing

Say, for example, you need a heading for a section on the critical importance of "saying what you mean." Call it something like "Superaccomplishment through Saying What You Mean" and you begin to capture something of the material's excitement.

10.2.3 Coin a New Word or Phrase

New words and combinations of words intrigue people. People read on, eager to see just how you explain yourself. If you are working on a section about how to "reduce company-wide error," take an extra few minutes to brainstorm. Look for a novel, colorful, and—above all—unique way to phrase your ideas. A few years ago, one management specialist did. He reached millions of readers and communicated the freshness and excitement of his program by writing about "Establishing a 'Zero Defects' Program."

10.2.4 Make a Bold Promise

Give readers hope of improvement. "Lower Cholesterol in Just Eight Weeks" dangles benefits like bait on a hook. Nothing strengthens reader interest like knowing what's in it for them.

10.2.5 Keep Headings Upbeat

People who turn to self-help/how-to books are looking for positive approaches to doing things right. If your goal is to discourage people from having affairs, you will certainly want to familiarize your readers with the destructive consequences of adultery. But it is still possible to present that information with a positive spin with a headline that announces, "Ten Good Reasons Not to Have an Office Affair."

Headings are another one of the many fun parts of writing a book. They offer you a challenge, stimulation, and a break from writing plain old text.

10.3   Five Steps to Dynamic Headings

This five-step strategy is guaranteed to produce clear, creative, effective headings:

1.   Review your sample chapter.

2. Look for major themes that might deserve headings. If you already have headings, review them. Either way, start with the first one.
3. Ask yourself what the main topic of the section is. Distill it in a few words. Presto! Heading.
4. Evaluate your heading against the list in Section 10.2. Is it written in everyday language? Is it intriguing and positive? Does it make a promise or offer a provocative new phrase?
5. When you are satisfied with what you've done, go on to the next section in your chapter and devise a heading for it.

10.4   The Lowdown on Subheadings

Sometimes you may have a major idea that deserves a heading and several components that you feel also need to be highlighted in a heading. In this case, by all means go ahead. Give them their own headings, too. These secondary headings are called *subheadings*. Once in a while, a subcomponent will have a sub-subcomponent of its own worthy of a heading, and so on. Usually you only need one or two levels of headings in a book, but if you need more, don't hold back. Use as many as it takes to highlight all your main ideas.

When there is more than one level of heading, publishing professionals designate these as A-heads, B-heads, C-heads, D-heads, and so forth (or 1-heads, 2-heads, 3-heads, 4-heads, etc.).

10.5   Differentiating Headings and Subheadings

Type headings, subheadings, sub-subheadings, and so on in different styles. It's important that the readers, and your publisher's typesetters, understand which headings designate major subjects and which designate their components (but keep them in the same font if you use a computer).

To differentiate headings and subheadings, type them in the following styles:

A-HEADS—FLUSH LEFT (EVEN WITH THE MARGIN). USE ALL CAPITAL LETTERS

B-Heads—Flush Left. First Letter of Each Major Word Capitalized

C-heads—Flush left. First letter of first word capitalized

<u>D-heads—Flush left and underlined. First letter of first word capitalized</u>

E-heads. Short heading in italics, indented and run in to paragraph it heads. First letter of first word capitalized, set off by a period

For instance, when writing a chapter about major industries, you might devote a section to transportation and its various forms, each of which would deserve its own heading. Handle it like this:

TRANSPORTATION: AN ABUNDANCE OF CHOICES (A-head)

Automobiles: Freedom of the Highways (B-head)

Trains: Freedom of the Rails (B-head)

Aircraft: Freedom of the Skies (B-head)

Passenger planes: Business and family only hours away (C-head)

Cargo planes: Fresh food, 3,000 miles before dinner (C-head)

Private planes: The dream of flying like birds (C-head)

<u>Jets: Boosting yourself to the stars</u> (D-head)

<u>Gliders: On silent wings</u> (D-head)

<u>Props: The old way is still the best</u> (D-head)

Single engine. (E-head)

Multiple engine. (E-head)

Turbo prop. (E-head)

Note that the first word following a colon is capitalized.

10.6   *When to Use Headings and Subheadings*

Use headings and subheadings frequently and often. As a rule of thumb, alert readers with one each time you introduce a new idea. Give every significant change of subject within a chapter a heading.

11

Lists Made Easy

11.1 *Bulleted Lists—Making Facts Your Bull's-Eye*

Bulleted lists are short lists of key points with a dot (•) or asterisk (*) in front of them. Put a bullet before each item in a list, and it immediately draws reader attention.

At some point in your self-help/how-to book, you'll probably find yourself with a series of important ideas, steps, equipment, or other items you want to list. Sometimes you have a series of key points you want to summarize in a visually arresting way—so that readers can find and remember them better. Use a bulleted list to attract readers' attention and to help them remember these points or items. The reader's eyes will be drawn straight to that vertical line of bullets like an arrow to a bull's-eye. Bulleted lists also help readers locate important points when they look them up for later reference.

Bulleted lists appear frequently in this book. You have probably run across them before in magazines and other books. The little dot is called a *bullet*, presumably because of its resemblance to a bullet hole.

Formatting bulleted lists
1. Type a dot or asterisk, and skip a space.
2. Type the first item (usually a few words to a sentence).
3. Skip to the next line. Repeat until the list is finished.

11.2   *When to Use Bulleted Lists*

Use bullets as a number one reader-grabber. That vertical line of dots, each with what is obviously an important point beside it, proclaims that something exciting, exceptional, or worthy of special attention is listed there. Bulleted lists are a visual magnet. Readers are compelled to stop and study each item. They are eager to see whether what you have bulleted is as exciting as you make it look and whether it's something they really need to know.

Use bullets any time you want to do the following:

- Highlight a series of items too important to let get lost in a sentence.
- Preview a connected series of issues extending over several pages.

11.2.1 Highlight Buried Points

Suppose I were to tell you that the four most important ideas in this book so far are selling your book with a proposal and sample chapter, writing chapters heading by heading, developing a warm, supportive style, and using bulleted lists. The information would be buried in a dense paragraph—lost among a welter of other words, ideas, and sentences. Readers who skip through a book might miss it altogether; casual readers might not realize its significance.

But just look at the difference when I put the same information in a bulleted list and tell you that the four most important ideas up to this point in the book are the following:

- Selling your book with a proposal and sample chapter
- Writing chapters heading by heading
- Developing a warm, supportive style
- Using bulleted lists

See how a bulleted list makes essential ideas stand out? They help readers zero in on the key elements. They shout, "Stop and look at this; this is different, so give it your full attention." Even the most casual browser can't help but notice them.

11.2.2 Preview a Connected Series of Issues

In a self-help/how-to book, you often will find yourself discussing a series of connected issues that extend over several pages. You may even have a heading for each. But readers will not notice the connection unless you point it out to them first, just as I did with this section and the one preceding it.

Case Histories and Quotations

12.1 Using Case Histories and Anecdotal Stories to Strengthen Reader Identification

Case histories and anecdotal stories illustrate important ideas with accounts of people who are just like the reader. Readers will understand points you make faster and visualize instructions more readily than with just a plain presentation of facts.

Case histories and anecdotes are really the same. Both are short accounts of ordinary people, just like the reader, that dramatize the ideas in your book. The term *case history* was originally applied to stories about patients in books by doctors and psychologists. *Anecdote* is a less formal term for stories about people that help explain ideas. To simplify things, I am going to refer to both as *anecdotal stories*.

Consider portraying what you are saying with an anecdote any time you need to do the following:

- Illustrate points and principles in action.
- Inspire people with the belief that they can successfully apply the ideas in your book.
- Motivate readers to put to use the strategies and exercises you teach.

12.1.1 Illustrate

Use anecdotal stories any time you wish to demonstrate a technique or principle at work in real life. In a book on posttraumatic stress disorder, you might use one to show the symptoms wreaking havoc in someone's life. In a book on business management, you might need to illustrate the stages of decline a company goes through once it begins to lose its foothold.

12.1.2 Inspire and Motivate

Inspire readers to try for themselves what you suggest. Share stories of those who have benefited from your program. Many readers will have even tried the advice given to them in other books without success. But when they read about people like themselves who have experienced healing and growth, readers become eager to see whether your approach will produce the same results in their own lives.

12.2 Writing Anecdotal Stories

Focus on keeping your anecdotal stories personable, memorable, and clearly embodying the points you wish to make. Follow the six steps below and you'll bring the people whose stories you tell to life and bring your points to the fore.

12.2.1 Introduce the Anecdote

Introduce the anecdote by explaining the idea or ideas it illustrates. Take a sentence or paragraph to explain what it means. Readers are more likely to remember both your anecdote and the points it makes if you introduce it this way. When readers know what elements are important ahead of time, they can focus more closely on the key points, without being distracted or confused by extraneous detail.

12.2.2 Use Names

Give names to the people in your stories. Anecdotes hit home harder when you give names to those you write about. "Fred Tolliver" and "Maria K." and "Li-Wong" sound like someone readers might know, giving your story realism and dimension. On the other hand, "a client of mine" seems anonymous. If you're writing about real people, however, don't use real names (see Section 12.4.2).

Embrace the widest possible audience by varying the ethnic backgrounds of the names you use. Ours is a multicultural nation. People seeking help come from many varied backgrounds. Everyone relates better to books when they find that people just like themselves are involved.

12.2.3 Characterize

Characterize by supplying important details about job or background. Give the reader (again, in brief) relevant information about the background of the subjects of any anecdotal stories you use. In a business book, describe their position or career path or even personal shortcomings that prevent them from progressing. Good openings include "Ramon G., in middle management at a large manufacturing corporation, had trouble working with those below him," or "Nicole, a vice president at a major airline," or "Yoko, a leading designer of women's clothing, found her company foundering."

In a book about adults suffering from the problems created by growing up in dysfunctional families, inform readers to what degree the family was dysfunctional. Say something like, "Rosario, whose mother drank heavily," or "Kristine B., whose stepfather molested her from the age of sixteen to twenty," or "Aaron, whose father was verbally abusive." These all convey information that provides crucial insights into the severity and direction of the person's difficulties.

112

In a how-to book for do-it-yourselfers remodeling their home, let readers know the degree of experience possessed by others who successfully followed your instructions—for example, "Joseph, who had never built anything before" or "Susan, who had made bird-houses but never tackled anything as demanding as remodeling an entire room." Each detail helps the reader realize that even novices can construct a new addition or remodel a home with little prior architectural or carpentry know-how.

12.2.4 Describe

Describe the subjects physically, if relevant. A person's physical appearance isn't generally crucial to an anecdote. After all, tall people can learn to tap into their intuition or apply communication skills to making an intimate relationship work just as effectively as short people. But in some instances, how a person looks or their age can materially aid a reader's understanding of an anecdote.

In medical case histories, the way someone looks can even provide important clues to knowledgeable physicians. Use descriptive phrases like "Katrinka, a woman whose swollen fingers suggested classic arthritis" or "Cristopher was a 56-year-old executive. His color was poor and his breathing labored as he sat in my office chair." These descriptions bring the individual to life and provide vital information that will illuminate a doctor's diagnosis and treatment of the case.

Appearance can also be relevant in describing those whose problems are more psychological than physiological. Such a description can provide a striking contrast, for instance, between someone's physical condition before a fitness training program and afterward. Describe "Anna" as "pale, thin, sickly" when we first meet her. Later, following your training program, portray her as "strong, muscular, and fit." In just a few short words, you have told readers a great deal about how getting into shape has changed her life for the better.

12.2.5 Recap

Recap the main idea or points it illustrated. For instance, if your anecdote illustrated the steps of reconciliation a couple must take to save a relationship, be sure to include a line or paragraph explaining and highlighting which elements of the story you want the reader to remember.

12.3 Keep It Short and Focused

Hold anecdotes to a manageable length. Condense them to somewhere between a paragraph and two manuscript pages. Focus them on portraying a single, strong idea or technique. Most people can only remember and concentrate on a few key ideas at a time. Long anecdotes that illustrate multiple points are harder for readers to follow and retain.

12.4 Use Multiple Anecdotes

Variety is important, too. Use several short anecdotes, involving different people, in each chapter. The greater the variety of character and background in these accounts, the greater the likelihood a reader will find one to identify with. The greater a reader's identification with the material in your chapters, the more he or she will retain it—and the greater his or her motivation to finish the book and apply it.

12.5 Actual Stories or "Composite" Stories?

Should you use anecdotes about actual people or combine them into "composite" cases? The following tips will help you decide which is best for your book—and when.

12.5.1 Pros and Cons

Knowing that every word of a case history is authentic lends it credibility with readers, but actual case histories don't always illustrate exactly what you want illustrated, the way you want it illustrated. When that happens, using a composite story designed to highlight your key points is the best solution. The following comparison chart contrasts the strengths and weaknesses of both.

Pros and Cons of Composite Stories

Composite	*Actual*
Pro	Pro
• Enables you to disguise actual individuals.	• Reassures readers your system worked on real people.
• Allows you to select just the elements that make the point.	
Con	Con
• Lacks a certain immediacy.	• Doesn't always illustrate every point you make.

12.5.2 Disguising Real People

When you choose to use anecdotes involving actual individuals, "change the names to protect the innocent." Don't embarrass clients or friends or run legal and ethical risks by giving away their real identities in your anecdote. Protect their anonymity by simply changing a few vital identifying background details.

1. Begin by altering the person's name. Make Susan Putney into Ruth Green.
2. Next, modify the name of the state they hail from. Transform Pennsylvanians into Michiganders, New Mexicans into Alabamians, or Louisianians into Oregonians.

3. Vary other details, when possible. Keep a woman at a similar level in the hierarchy, but switch the company's business from tractors to scythes. Or turn a slender blond woman into a portly brunette. Or you might even change gender—a woman from a broken home might become a man from one.

Of course, there will be times when distinctive, specific details of the person's past life, profession, or gender are crucial to the point you are making. Position in a company hierarchy, family background, medical history, and many other particulars can prove relevant. When this is the case, go ahead and use the true details, but just remember to vary all the details that aren't essential to understanding the story.

12.5.3 Creating Composites

Follow these guidelines for creating successful composite case anecdotes:

1. Jot down the points you want to make in the story.
2. Review all the people you have known who fit the profile for use in your anecdote. Draw anecdotes from their lives that reflect those points.
3. Select elements and arrange facts into a single story that illustrates the points you are making.

Composite stories may seem less trouble to write, because you can select just the elements you want, but be warned—they still require careful thought. Rearranging the facts in a way that best illustrates the point you are making can cause an anecdote to sound too perfect to be believable.

The rule here is: Don't make your anecdotes too "happily ever after" perfect. No one's life becomes instantly better, nor is every single problem solved, no matter how effective a program. Nor does everyone get every technique, principle, and rule right the first time. Acknowledge this when you include a composite story. Let the readers know that the people in your anecdotes encountered difficulty and made mistakes when they began to try out your advice. Then describe the success that perseverance brought. Show that even after mastering ten steps to recovery from heart disease, or ten steps to a power golf swing, there were still new challenges to meet, from within and without, new skills to learn, new aspects of life to face and conquer for the people in your stories.

12.6   If You Must Use Quotations

In those instances where real names *must* be used—in the case of an interview or testimonial within the text, for example—be sure that the individual signs a release form authorizing the use of his or her own words. Your publisher should supply the forms to you after your book contract is signed. If the publisher forgets, make sure you request the forms yourself.

12.6.1   Using Quotations Effectively

Sometimes, you will have an apt quotation from other writers or authorities you feel would add the perfect touch to your text. This may be an arresting statistic, an insightful observation, or simply something said so well that paraphrasing would not do justice to the point you're trying to make.

A half dozen to a dozen (or more) such quotations per chapter establishes that you have studied widely in your area of expertise. This helps underscore your credibility by proving that your own ideas are built on a solid foundation of knowledge. (Of course, in some circumstances, you may need to secure permission to use quotations from other writers and publications; these are covered in Chapter 18.)

As with case histories, it's usually a good idea to tell readers why you are using a particular quotation before you use it. When readers know what the point of a quotation will be, they'll understand it more fully. Generally, all it takes to introduce one is a sentence, but it's an all-important sentence that ensures that readers will get the most out of the quotation you use.

12.6.2 How to Attribute Quotes

Here's the proper way to cite sources and authors in a self-help/how-to book: Don't cite them the way you do in academic works and papers. Instead, look at the way quotations from other sources are used in newspapers, magazines, and other bestselling self-help/how-to books. The idea is to just identify the author(s) and the book, publication, or specific article title. Classic approaches include the following: "According to Dr. Mary Schwartz, of Miskatonic University Medical School, writing in *Cosmopolitan*" or "'Try a more informal approach,' suggests John Lewis Tracy, head of the Boston Clinic for Spendaholics."

Forget listing volume numbers, page references, footnotes, publishers, and other academic baggage. These reader turnoffs belong in a notes or bibliography section at the back of the book (see Chapter 21). When most people see those types of citations in a book, they decide it's a work for professionals or academics and over their heads. They put it back on the shelf and search for one that seems written for people like them.

Now that you have learned to breeze through most of the basic elements that make a bestselling chapter, it's time to finish off by discovering the tricks that make using exercises, quizzes, and checklists easy, too.

13

Checklists, Quizzes, Exercises, and Other Interactive Elements

13.1 Interactive Elements—The Heart of Your Self-Help/How-To Book

Strategies and techniques that empower people to make positive changes in their lives are the foundation of any successful self-help/how-to book. These "interactive" elements are the heart of your book, the elements that make it "self-help." They are the parts of your book that provide explicit, step-by-step, easy-to-follow guidance in putting your program into action. It is the interactive elements that convince readers to buy self-help/how-to books.

People are mostly passive when reading a self-help/how-to book, but strategies, guidelines, exercises, checklists, quizzes, and journaling call for the reader's own participation. People stop being passive and begin to interact with your book. These elements do the following:

- Get readers actively involved with your book.
- Actually solve problems or expand skills.
- Strengthen the readers' sense of their abilities, rather than disabilities.

"The essence of a practical book," one world-famous publisher advises self-help/how-to authors, "lies in what-to-do and how-to-do-it information, with plenty of illustrative examples and specific steps for the reader to follow."

13.2   A Checklist of Interactive Elements

Here's the easy way to decide whether a quiz, checklist, or exercise is the best choice. You may already have decided on the interactive elements you plan to use. But if you are still in the early stages of planning your book—or find yourself stuck for just the right way to help the readers acquire an insight or skill—use the following checklist to spark your thinking. Each has unique properties; each is ideal for a different task.

It isn't possible to provide a comprehensive list of every type of interactive element self-help/how-to authors have put in their books. There are dozens, perhaps hundreds, of possible variations. I've used many of them in this book. Feel free to adapt those that follow to suit your own specific needs.

☐   *Checklist.*   Takes the form of a numbered or bulleted list—or one with boxes that the reader can check. Use a checklist when you want to assist readers in making a determination about something: whether they have a specific problem, whether they are applying a system correctly, whether they have remembered a series of important ideas, and so on.

☐   *Comparison list.*   Takes the form of two or more columns contrasting the descriptions contained in one column with the descriptions contained in the other(s). Use a comparison list when you want to contrast two or more conditions. They are often used to compare negative versus positive qualities, but you can use them to compare differences in almost anything: healthy as compared with unhealthy behavior, what things are like at different stages of development, the behavior of women and men, effective and ineffective management, normal and creative states of consciousness, myths versus facts, closeness and real intimacy, and so on.

☐ *Fill-in-the-blank list.* Takes the form of an incomplete question, phrase, sentence, or paragraph with a blank line where the reader can write a response. Use this when you want to steer people toward important self-discoveries by making them more aware of their thoughts, feelings, attitudes, fantasies, and actions. Fill in the blank takes a number of forms:

- *Complete the sentence*: A sentence with a missing word or phrase to be filled in.
- *Finish a statement*: Provides the opening of a statement, followed by blank lines for the reader to fill in.
- *Describe a situation or answer a question*: Use for longer, more reflective material. Although there is a blank line in the book, the reader is invited to use a sheet of paper and take as much space as needed to complete a response.

☐ *Couple exercises.* Takes the form of exercises and strategies intended to get partners involved with actively understanding and bettering their relationship. Use when you want to get readers working together to improve intimacy, communication, problem solving, romance, power sharing, and other common problems that give duos difficulty. (These are often variants of the other interactive elements described in this checklist.)

☐ *Guidelines.* Takes the form of a concise list of rules. Use guidelines when you want to provide guidance on how to do something more effectively, things to avoid, how to determine whether something is healthy or unhealthy, and so on.

☐ *Journaling.* Takes the form of a written journal, where the reader answers questions requiring lengthy answers or records certain kinds of thoughts, feelings, and/or activities. Use journaling when you want to help the reader gain critical self-insights, chart personal growth, or learn new ways of looking at the world.

☐ *Physical exercises.* Takes the form of detailed, usually numbered, instructions. Use these when you want to lead the reader through the steps involved in any physical activity. Typically used for the following:

- Sports
- Do-it-yourself
- Exercise
- Weight reduction
- Releasing emotions or promoting positive feelings
- Crafts
- Enhancing sexuality

☐ *Quiz.* Takes the form of items the reader is challenged to react to or questions he or she is challenged to answer. Use when you want to ensure that the reader remembers key ideas or anytime you want to engender self-discovery and insights. There are many kinds of quizzes:

- Multiple choice
- True or false
- Boxes to check
- Scores to add up

☐ *Role-playing.* Takes the form of acting out the role of another and responding as he or she might respond (often an influential parent, the reader as a child, or even specific aspects of his or her personality [the critical self, the creative self, the organized self, the successful self]). Use role-playing when you want to help readers gain critical self-insight or put them in touch with critical aspects of their personality. Role-playing can also include two-chair dialogues, where the reader carries on a conversation by speaking as him- or herself while sitting in one chair, and the other person while sitting in the second chair.

☐ *Strategies.* Takes the form of formulas for handling difficult situations. Use these when you want to provide the reader with an overall approach to anything problematic, whether golf, geriatrics, or growth.

☐ *Visualization.* Takes the form of intensely building up a mental image. This is based on the scientific discovery that imagining something, like the taste of a lemon or our most triumphant moment, produces profound physical and psychological changes. Use it to help readers acquire new skills, transform self-defeating attitudes, or draw on deep wells of wisdom, healing, and inner strength. Visualization has a multitude of applications:

- *Accessing inner wisdom:* Opens doorways to the subconscious, allowing us to tap our deepest source of creativity and inspiration.
- *Emotional healing:* Promotes calmness and deep relaxation, and soothes our "inner child."
- *Health and healing:* Enhances the immune system, directs blood flow to injured areas, eases pain and stress, and promotes health and well-being.
- *Mental rehearsal:* Mentally prepares someone for difficult and challenging events in sports, business, and personal life.
- *Reprogramming self-defeating attitudes:* Transforms negative attitudes and self-destructive or compulsive behaviors and feelings, overcomes fears and phobias, and enhances motivation and self-esteem.

13.3 Making Interactive Elements "Just Like Being There"

Use this surefire strategy to generate reader-friendly quizzes, checklists, strategies, and exercises. In real life, when you give a client or workshop participant instructions for doing something, you are present to clarify questions or misunderstandings. But you won't be there when someone is reading your book, so you want to be sure the instructions for interactive elements are so crystal clear that even the most easily confused reader can follow them.

You also need to anticipate and answer all the possible questions or misunderstandings people might have (just reflect on what participants at lectures and workshops have asked you). In other words, you want to give readers as complete an understanding of what to do, how to do it, and what it all means as they would get if they were at a presentation given by you.

When it comes to creating effective interactive elements, there's one simple key: detail, detail, and more detail—that is, detailed instructions at the beginning, detailed instructions in the middle, and detailed instructions at the end. Keep this formula in mind. It's a potent three-step method for producing interactive elements, instructions, and techniques so clear and thorough that you answer all the readers' questions—before they ask them.

Use these three simple steps to develop powerful, effective interactive elements:

1. *Explain how and why the technique works* and what it will do for the reader. Naturally, many readers will have doubts about their ability to do the exercises and correctly use the strategies in your book. Some have tried other books, therapies, systems, and approaches before without success and are justifiably uncertain about whether yours will do what you claim. We also live in a very cynical age, one that automatically makes people skeptical about much of what they are told and promised.

   But you can convince readers to give you a try by explaining the what, why, and how of every interactive element. So before writing a word on any quiz, checklist, or exercise, stop and spell out for the reader the following:

   What

   Describe what it will do for the reader, the specific benefit, skill, or insight that will be gained: a more effective follow-through on a golf swing, an accurate assessment of how serious a problem might be, improved sexual communication between partners, or a list of necessary equipment.

Why

Describe why it will do what you claim, the reason it produces the benefit: the way the twist of a wrist adds torsion to a swing, or the way using sentences focused on your own feelings and needs rather than on blaming a partner will allow your partner to hear your message instead of becoming defensive.

How

To strengthen motivation, detail how each technique will benefit the reader.

2. *Spell out how to do the quiz, exercise, or other interactive element in minute detail.* Break down each element into as many steps and substeps as necessary. The more fully you describe what to do and how to do it, the easier you make your instructions to understand and follow. The simpler it is, the more willing readers will be to give it a try. (You will find dozens of examples in this book.)

3. *Tell the reader how he or she should interpret the results or be different after completing it.* When an element is evaluative (quiz, write-in, journaling, couple exercises, etc.), explain fully how to apply or understand the information generated. Or, if it is designed to impart a skill or heal a wound or improve life, try to impart some sense of how the reader might feel afterward or how life might be different.

Part Five

Self-Editing Self-Help/
How-To Books

Editing Your Manuscript the Lazy Writer's Way

14.1 Editing Your First Draft Like a Pro

Most beginning writers labor for weeks over editing a chapter, trying to get it right. Even then, they may miss critical shortcomings that a more objective eye would spot. With the pair of powerful tools you will get in this chapter and the next—"The Lazy Writer's Self-Editing Checklist" and "The Manuscript Troubleshooting List for Your Friends," you can breeze through the entire process of polishing and perfecting your sample chapter—and every other chapter—in no time. These two tools will give you everything you need to edit your manuscripts like a professional.

The Self-Editing Checklist will help you quickly spot elements and qualities you may have left out of your chapter or that might benefit from improvement. Use the checklist when you have finished the first draft of a chapter or an entire book. After you have spotted and fixed every weakness you can locate, turn the manuscript over to several friends. Have them vet what you have written using the Manuscript Troubleshooting Checklist in the following chapter.

14.2   How to Use the Lazy Writer's Self-Editing Checklist

First, apply this checklist to your sample chapter. Later, use it to self-edit all your chapters.

The Lazy Writer's Self-Editing Checklist is a three-step process that enables you to detect and correct the common defects that cause publishers to reject books. But your manuscript won't be rejected, because with the Self-Editing Checklist you will have eliminated those flaws like a pro, long before your publisher sees it. Here's how to use the checklist:

1. Study each item on the checklist.
2. Review each page of your chapter and look for instances where a rule might be applied. When you believe you have found a problematic area, study it carefully. If you find the section can be changed for the better, make a note.
3. Go over these notes when you finish reviewing the chapter.
4. Revise the chapter using your notes as your guide.

14.3   The Lazy Writer's Self-Editing Checklist

To troubleshoot manuscripts easily, let the following checklist keep track of the details for you. During my years in trade publishing, I discovered that most beginning self-help/how-to authors made the same mistakes. Later, when asked to lead workshops at writers' conferences, I compiled a list of these blunders for distribution to participants. I called this the Self-Editing Checklist. It enabled novice writers to pinpoint and avoid typical beginners' errors. The response was so enthusiastic that I decided to share this list with you (tear out or copy the list).

☐ *Case histories.* Have you introduced the case history fully and characterized each person involved? (Chapter 12)

☐ *Condensing.* Is there any place the manuscript seems to go on about one subject too long and might benefit from condensation?

☐ *Cross-references.* Have you referred your readers to related materials in other chapters (as I have throughout this book)? This will be especially helpful to those who only read the chapters that apply to their own particular concerns. (Chapter 20)

☐ *Definitions.* Have you defined every term? Look for any words the reader might not find familiar.

☐ *Examples.* Is there any place where you feel it would be easier for the reader to understand an idea if it were illustrated by an example? Explain how something works or how someone behaves.

☐ *Exercises.* Have you introduced each exercise fully, explained the steps in sufficient detail, and shown readers what changes to expect in their lives? (Chapter 13)

☐ *Explanations.* Are there any important, technical, or unfamiliar ideas or concepts that you haven't fully explained?

☐ *Facts.* Have you double-checked all dates, statistics, attributions, and other facts? Memory is not very reliable.

☐ *Focus.* Have you stuck to the main topic throughout a chapter or section? Are there any tangents or hobby horses? (Chapter 8)

☐ *Headings and subheadings.* Are they uniform? Pertinent? Suitable? (Chapter 10)

☐ *Introductions.* Have you introduced chapters, sections, and subsections fully *before* discussing the main ideas? (Chapter 8)

☐ *Negative comparisons.* Have you inadvertently explained only what something is not rather than what it is? Any time you discover you have written about what something isn't, look back to see whether you have also explained what it is.

☐ *Organization.* Can you find any material you feel (1) should go earlier or later in a chapter, (2) belongs in a different chapter, or (3) is scattered throughout the text and should be drawn together in its own section?

☐ *Proportions.* Have you given more space to big issues and briefer treatment to smaller ones?

☐ *Quizzes.* Have you explained how to use and how to interpret each? (Chapter 13)

☐ *Reader involvement.* Have you consistently remembered to write the reader into the book? Is the reader addressed frequently enough through the use of "you"? (Chapter 9)

☐ *Repetition.* Are there any places where you notice unnecessary repetition? Look for recurring words, phrases, and ideas that you could eliminate.

☐ *Run-on sentences.* Do you have any sentences of three lines or longer? If you can revise what you're saying into two sentences, you probably should.

☐ *Technical terms.* Have you eliminated or explained all technical, professional, clinical, or other unusual words or terms that might be unfamiliar to some readers? (Chapter 9)

☐ *Theme.* Is the theme of the chapter clear as well as how it relates to the overall theme of your book? (Chapter 8)

☐ *Tighten flaccid writing.* Are there places where you have become too wordy? If you can condense six words into three words (or less) without changing the meaning, you probably should.

Getting Friends to Troubleshoot and Edit Your Manuscript

15.1 *How Friends Can Help Make Your Book a Bestseller*

Here's the easiest way of all to troubleshoot manuscripts: Get friends to do it for you. It's easier for others to see our mistakes than it is for us to spot them.

An article about John Creasey, one of the world's bestselling mystery authors, introduced me to this system. Creasey turned out one book a month, every month—twelve titles a year—every one a critical and financial success.

With a production schedule like that, Creasey obviously didn't have time to troubleshoot his own first drafts. He also knew fresh eyes would detect flaws he might miss. Creasey's solution was to send every manuscript to a group of friends. He asked them to make notes about where they felt the book fell short and might be improved. The books Creasey revised this way became bestselling novels.

One how-to author uses a variation of this which became a surefire technique for ensuring that each chapter stands on its own and can be understood without reference to the others. When a book is finished, she hosts a small party for friends willing to read and criticize her manuscript. She hands each guest a chapter to pick apart for errors. None of her friends know what is in the rest of the book. If she finds they don't understand something that relates to material elsewhere in the book, she revises the passage to make it complete in itself.

Another successful self-help/how-to author uses a variant of this approach that gets the job done without delay as soon as he finishes each chapter. He invites selected friends to dinner. Afterward, he reads them the material and asks for comments. Because they are in a group, his friends are less afraid to speak freely, and he gets the frank no-nonsense criticism he needs to polish his chapters to perfection.

15.1.1 The Reader Is Always Right

One reason this system works so well is that it's based on a principle every businessperson knows. The customer is always right. The reader is always right, too. Experienced authors realize that if a reader doesn't understand something you wrote, or isn't sure what your broader point is, or is confused, or is bored—the reader is right. Professionals know you can't argue with that.

You won't be around to clarify a misunderstood point or shorten a passage that runs too long when people are reading your book at home. But you won't have to worry. Give friends the troubleshooting list below. Let your friends identify areas that readers are likely to find confusing, boring, or poorly developed. Then fix them yourself, while your book is still in manuscript form. By the time your book reaches readers, you will have located and addressed all their possible questions and concerns—and your friends will have done the job for you.

15.1.2 One Step to a Zero-Defect Book

When it comes to polishing the final draft of a manuscript, friends are one of your most valuable resources. They can add an extra eye to help you identify weaknesses. Friends also add a more objective eye; they can see where a point is abstruse enough that a case history or an example would enhance the reader's understanding or where you have gone on too long pursuing a favorite topic.

There's one more way friends can help. They can also point out the parts of your manuscript they think work especially well. Once you know what you do best, you can look for other places where you could apply those skills and ideas when revising the manuscript. This improves the book overall, helping to bring it up to your highest level of workmanship.

You don't even have to dream up questions to ask your friends. The Manuscript Troubleshooting Checklist provides over one dozen problem areas that editors and authors look for when they trouble-shoot manuscripts. I've even made it easy for your friends by adding a list of abbreviations I use when working on manuscripts myself. (You can use them when reviewing your own work.)

When you have finished troubleshooting your book with the Lazy Writer's Self-Editing Checklist and the Manuscript Trouble-shooting List for Your Friends, you can submit your work with confidence—knowing you have done everything any professional author can to perfect a manuscript.

15.2 About the Manuscript Troubleshooting List for Your Friends

The Manuscript Troubleshooting Checklist arose out of a comment that many first-time authors make to editors in cover letters. Over and over these writers reported that their "friends had loved the book." In discussions of cover letters during writing workshops, I told participants point-blank to avoid mentioning friends' endorsements. I concluded by observing, "Of course they'll say they like it. If they value your friendship, and are aware of the effort you put in— what are they going to do? Tell you they hate it?"

But knowing that authors would continue to pester friends into reading their manuscripts, I asked myself how friends could actually contribute to the writing process. Mostly what editors do is act as the reader's researcher, looking for material that is unclear, that seems off the subject, that lacks interest, or that otherwise might be improved. Why couldn't friends do the same?

Don't ask your friends whether they liked the book, I began to advise authors. Instead, ask them what they disliked. Again, I worked up a handout listing problematic areas that friends could keep an eye out for while reading the author's book. The result was the Manuscript Troubleshooting List for Your Friends.

15.3   How to Use the Manuscript Troubleshooting List for Your Friends

Give this list to friends. Ask them to use it while they read your manuscript. It will enable them to supply quality feedback in two simple steps:

1. Quickly review the list to familiarize themselves with the kinds of problem areas professional editors look for.
2. Use the abbreviations the list provides to mark the manuscript wherever they feel they have detected one of those problems.

When you get the marked-up manuscript back from friends, review it carefully. Consider their comments and make whatever changes and improvements you feel are warranted.

Of course, your friends aren't experts, but anytime two or more have the same problem with your book, you can be sure that some of your intended readers will have the same problem, too. In the final analysis, you must decide which of their comments are valid yourself, but you can't go wrong by heeding their advice as often as possible.

15.4 The Manuscript Troubleshooting List for Your Friends

Tear out or copy the list.

_/   = This passage, idea, or phrase is particularly good or has strong emotional impact.

*   = This is exceptional.

Awk   = Awkwardly expressed, could be more smoothly written.

Bor   = Bored me.

Con   = Subject goes on too long and could benefit from being shortened or condensed.

Cut   = This material seems too far off from the point of the book or chapter and might well be deleted without impairing the reader's understanding of the main theme(s).

Def   = Please define this term or phrase; I'm not sure everyone will be familiar with it.

Dev   = This is an important point that deserves greater development.

Earlier = This material should go earlier where it would illuminate what you have been saying better or because the main body of the material on this subject is there. (Indicate where the material should be moved, if possible.)

Exm   = This idea would benefit from being illustrated by an example.

Exp   = Explaining this idea more fully would help make it clearer or give it greater impact.

Gr   = A problem with grammar.

I/L   = I'm lost and don't see either where the material is going, or how it relates to my life, or how it relates to the theme of the book or chapter.

137

Jar = Too jargonistic and filled with professional or academic terminology.

NC = Not clear to me.

Pl = Material seems out of place here; doesn't appear to be part of the main sequence of thought. (If you have an idea of where it actually belongs—earlier or later in a chapter, or in a different chapter, or perhaps with other material scattered throughout the book that deserves a section of its own—write "Move to [and the page or chapter where you feel it belongs].)

Rep = Unnecessarily repetitive.

Sp = A misspelled word. (Circle the suspect word.)

T/B = Too textbookish and academic in phraseology or approach.

Tr = Some kind of transition is needed here; the switch of topics was confusing or the relation between this idea and the one that preceded it is not clear.

W/S = Why is this so? Explain why it is the way you say it is, or why it works the way it does.

Weak = Weak material; seems as if it could be improved or made stronger.

WYM = The point of this material or how it connects with the subject at hand isn't clear—why are you telling me this?

Part Six

Selling Self-Help/How-To
Books Made Easy

Submitting Your Book for Publication

16.1 *How to Find a Publisher*

Don't let submitting or selling your book to publishers intimidate you. They are looking for well-crafted self-help/how-to proposals. The real question is how to best get your proposal to them. As a credentialed self-help/how-to author or collaborator, you have two options:

1. Send the proposal to publishers yourself.
2. Find a literary agent who will attend to the details.

There are advantages and disadvantages to both, but my advice is let an agent do it for you.

16.2 *Submitting through a Literary Agent*

Let me reiterate: Getting an agent is the best and easiest way to go. Why do something yourself when there are more qualified people eager to do the job for you and who can do it better? There are two critical reasons why it's to your advantage to have an agent handle your book.

1. Agents are in touch with editors on a daily basis and know their areas of interest and expertise. They can direct your proposal straight to the most likely buyer. Often, an agent can sell your book the first time out, whereas if you submit it yourself, the process might take much longer.
2. Editors respect agents. If a literary agent they know says that your proposal is special, most editors will give reading it a high priority.

Some authors forgo agents for attorneys. But, with all due respect to these able ladies and gentlemen, I still recommend an agent. Because they keep such close tabs on the literary world, agents know more about negotiating contracts—and more about how much a particular publisher is likely to pay for your book—than even the most experienced literary attorney. Agents also have representatives in other countries whose job is to sell translation and other foreign rights for your book.

Most agents charge 15 percent of your advance and of all subsequent earnings from direct sales, domestic and foreign, of your book. This is a bargain. Your agent will earn you far more than that, through both changes they negotiate in your contract and the sale of magazine, book club, translation, and other subsidiary rights, as they are called.

The *Literary Market Place* (along with other books in the Recommended Reading section) lists literary agents and whether they handle self-help/how-to books. Like publishers, most agents stay on the lookout for self-help/how-to proposals, because they're popular with readers. But some literary agents concentrate their efforts in very limited areas and won't take on a self-help/how-to project. You'll save yourself time and postage if you avoid sending material to agents who are not going to be interested in your work. Look up some likely agents and mail your proposal and sample chapter to them.

16.3 Submitting the Book Yourself

Even submitting your book yourself is relatively easy. If you have expertise of any kind in your subject area—or are collaborating with someone who does—most publishers will take your proposal as seriously as one that comes from an agent. Finding the names of interested publishers isn't hard. Most big libraries carry *Literary Market Place*, which lists publishers, the types of books they specialize in, and even the names of their editors. (You will find more on the LMP, as publishing insiders call it, and other guides to U.S. and foreign publishers, in the Recommended Reading section at the end of this book.)

The major drawback to directly submitting your proposal without a literary agent is that it might not reach the one editor at a publishing company who would really respond to its potential. Because editors differ as much as writers, this can be a key factor in determining the acceptance or rejection of your manuscript. You are submitting the book blind as far as editors go.

Also, negotiating book contracts is a fine art. All the big publishers are honest and their contracts fair—they want to keep authors, not alienate them. But an expert agent can obtain subtle changes that, over the course of your book's life, might place thousands of more dollars in your pocket. Moreover, agents can often wangle extras you would never have thought of, like a bonus when your book appears on the bestseller list. (If you do opt to take on the task of submitting your manuscript directly, you will find several works on negotiating book contracts listed in the Recommended Reading section.)

Putting Your Manuscript in Professional Form

17.1 *Giving Your Book the Professional Look*

Impress publishers and agents with your professionalism at first sight. Put your proposal as well as your whole manuscript when completed— in fact, everything you submit for publication—in proper manuscript form. There's nothing complicated about it.

Formatting manuscripts
Here's how to format your manuscript professionally:

- Double-space the entire manuscript (i.e., a line skipped between each line of text).
- Have approximately twenty-five lines per page, approximately sixty-six characters per line.
- Type on one side of white bond paper (no erasable paper) only. If you're using a computer, printing on a laser or ink-jet printer is preferable. A near-letter-quality dot matrix printer may be OK, but avoid regular dot matrix—it's too hard to read, and some publishers won't accept it. If you're a typewriter diehard, use a good, black ribbon.

- Use regular pica font (if using a computer, use standard 12-point Courier).
- Place your last name, the title of the book, the chapter number and title, and the page number in every upper left-hand corner.
- Use one-inch margins at the top, bottom, and sides of the page. As with typing double-spaced, this may seem like a waste of paper, but there's sound reasoning behind it. Publishers need space on the sides and between the lines for copyediting marks.
- Provide a separate title page, also containing your name and mailing address.
- Clearly label all elements.
- Number all pages sequentially, beginning with the title page.

When your manuscript arrives in the correct form, publishers perceive you as a writing professional from the start. This gives you the inside track over most beginners. Your book will be ready for consideration, whereas others will be returned with a set of guidelines on proper manuscript preparation.

17.2 One Last Sales Tip Before Packaging Your Book for Submission

Guarantee your book an eager reading from agents and publishers by adding a hot cover letter. Make it exciting by distilling your theme, approach, and benefits into a single page. (You acquired all the skills you need in Chapter 5, while writing your proposal.)

Describe your book in a dramatic paragraph. Briefly state your theme, approach, the benefits that readers will acquire, and how large a readership will be interested in your book. In another paragraph, highlight your credentials and, remember, don't be shy. Make yourself sound like someone qualified to write your book.

17.3 Packaging Your Book for Delivery

The following checklists include every step in preparing your book for mailing. Follow these steps carefully, whether it's your proposal or your finished manuscript. Place your cover letter on top. Slip a large rubber band or binder clip around everything. Do not bind your manuscript or proposal. Editors hate to work with manuscripts that are bound in any way because they must be disassembled for editing and copying.

Put your manuscript in a carton or envelope. Enclose a self-addressed envelope, with return postage prepaid. Then send it to the first agent or publisher on your list.

17.3.1 Proposal Submission Checklist

The Proposal Submission Checklist makes it easy to remember all the elements you may want to include when assembling your proposal for submission:

- [ ] A cover letter
- [ ] A title page with your name and address
- [ ] An overview
- [ ] A "Comparison" page
- [ ] A "Target Audience" page
- [ ] A "Marketing" page
- [ ] A "Promotion and Publicity" page
- [ ] An "Estimated Time of Completion" section
- [ ] A section estimating the length of the book
- [ ] A section listing nontextual information such as charts and illustrations
- [ ] An "About the Author" page

☐ A proposed table of contents

☐ A proposed chapter-by-chapter outline

☐ Photocopies of material about you

☐ A photograph of yourself

☐ A sample chapter, bearing the book and chapter title, along with your name

17.3.2 Completed Manuscript Checklist

Here's an easy way to make sure you don't leave anything out when you send your completed manuscript to the publisher for publication. Not all of these will apply to your book, but the complete list is offered so that you don't overlook anything vital:

☐ A cover letter, detailing anything special your publisher should know about format or material

☐ A list of captions for all figures, which may include photographs, illustrations, and charts (see Section 20.6)

☐ A title page with your name and address

☐ The title page of the book

☐ A dedication

☐ An acknowledgments section

☐ A permissions section

☐ A finalized table of contents

☐ A finalized chapter-by-chapter outline

☐ An introduction

☐ A preface

☐ An author's note

☐ Every chapter numbered sequentially

☐ Appendixes

☐ A recommended reading list

☐ A resources list

☐ A bibliography

☐ Notes

☐ References

☐ An index

☐ An "About the Author" page

Part Seven

Simplifying Permissions,
Cross-References, Illustrations,
Charts, Tables, and Front and
Back Matter

Permission to Quote and Reprint

18.1 It Only Sounds Complicated

You can relax right now. Permissions, references, illustrations, bibliographies, appendixes, and indexes are not complex and intimidating. They're a snap when you know the shortcuts. I describe them in some of the shortest chapters in the book.

Take permissions. Getting the okay to quote from other writers or reproduce illustrations is simple. Most publishers, music companies, photographers, and authors are eager to grant their permission. It's like a free advertisement for them. Once in a while, you may encounter an exception, but don't let it blight your day. You will probably find that your book can stand on its own without the material in question.

Occasionally, someone might require a small reprint fee. If you plan to quote extensively from other sources, ask your publisher in advance if they would be willing to help cover any costs involved.

One important note here: It is the author's, not the publisher's, responsibility to secure permission for use of text and artwork. Don't assume the publisher will handle it—most won't; and don't go ahead and use material without written permission in hand. Even though it is rare for permission to be denied, you don't want to have to make extensive revisions to your manuscript after it's been accepted for publication because you don't have the necessary permissions.

18.2 Getting Permissions—Let Them Do the Work For You

Here's an easy way to get permissions for material in books:

1. Write a list of all the material you believe might require permission to use (see Section 18.3).
2. Write a letter for each case exactly as follows:

```
Permissions Dept.
[Name of firm or individual]
[Mailing address]
[City, state, and zip code]
```

In re: Permission to reprint from [title if known]

Dear Permissions Department:

I am [your credential]. Currently I am writing a book on [subject], titled [title], for [publisher]. It is based on my years as [background] and is intended to help people who [topic of your book].

I would like permission to quote from [source of quotation] by [author's name if known].

I plan to quote from this work [number of times] in my text. The total wordage I will be quoting will be [number of] words.

The material I plan to quote can be found on [page number or numbers] of the [copyright year] edition. It begins with the phrase [opening phrase in quotes] and ends with [closing phrase in quotes].

I would like nonexclusive permission to use this
material throughout the world in my book cited
above.

Could you please tell me what procedure I need
to follow to secure this permission?

Sincerely,

[Your name]

3. Mail each letter, along with a self-addressed, stamped envelope, to the party from whom you are seeking permission.
If it's a firm, the permissions department will take care of
the rest. You will be provided with a permission form to fill
out. You will also be told whether you may reprint the passage
as a courtesy or a fee is required. If it's an individual, he or
she will let you know the particular requirement.

Vary the letter when seeking clearance for articles, songs, poems, records, photographs, drawings, charts, and everything else.

For *articles in periodicals and poems:* "I would very much like
permission to quote from [name of article] by [author's name]
from [title of publication with date or issue number]."

For *song lyrics:* "I would very much like permission to quote
from [name of song] by [song writer's name, if known, singer's
name if not] from [title of album, if known]."

A *note on poems and lyrics:* In the case of song lyrics and poems, tell how many lines you plan to use rather than the
number of words. You may even want to attach the portion
you will be quoting, because these are usually so brief.

For *illustrative material:* "I would very much like permission to
reproduce the [photograph, drawing, graph, advertisement,
chart, table, etc.] on page [page number] of [title of book or
publication, for a publication add date or number]."

18.3   When Do You Need Permission to Reproduce?

This may be the only tricky part of self-help/how-to writing. That's because it involves legal issues, which are always open to interpretation and reinterpretation in the courts. However, if you follow the general rules of thumb that prevail in publishing, you are unlikely to encounter difficulty. When in doubt, the best course is to consult your publisher; they have a legal department that can answer thorny questions involving copyrights and permissions.

18.3.1 For Illustrative Material

The following guidelines will help you determine whether you need permission to reprint a photograph, drawing, painting, chart, or other illustrative material that is currently in copyright. In practice, this breaks down into two very simple rules. Always get permission to reprint the following:

1.   Anything from the last twenty-eight years.
2.   Anything from the last seventy years that is from
     A major publication.
     A major artist or photographer.
     A major wire service.

18.3.2 For Printed Matter

The following guidelines will help you determine when you need permission to quote from books, articles, songs, poems, and the rest. You don't need permission to quote brief passages. This is known legally as the rules of *fair use*. Fair use means that it is okay to quote a few lines—even a paragraph or two to make a point—but don't abuse the privilege by an overreliance on the words of others to do your work for you. (For longer passages, the rules of copyright apply [see Section 18.3.1].)

You definitely need permission to reproduce the following:

- Anything that is complete and copyrightable in and of itself (map, chart, short poem, poster, cartoon strip, and so on).
- More than one line of a poem or popular song.
- More than three paragraphs in succession.
- Any material from a single article or book quoted more than half a dozen or more times.

18.4 Three More Tips for Trouble-Free Permissions

After years of gathering clearances for my own books, I've learned three rules that may help smooth your own permissions process:

- Start early.
- Look on the label.
- Ask your publisher for help.

18.4.1 Start Early

The best time to begin rounding up permissions is right after you sign your book contract. From that moment on, anytime you decide to use something you feel might require clearance, write off at once for permission to use it. Keep your permissions in a separate file. When you have received clearances for all the material you plan to incorporate into your book, photocopy your permissions and send the copies to your editor.

18.4.2 Where to Get Them—Look on the Label

It's usually pretty easy to tell who to contact for permissions. Here are two tips to get you started:

1. The names and addresses of publishers, along with copy-right dates, are given in the opening pages of most books and magazines.
2. The names and addresses of record companies usually appear on the covers of albums, cassettes, and CDs.

18.4.3 Ask Your Publisher for Help

When you encounter a problem with permissions, ask your publisher for help. You may not be able to find out who wrote the comic poem "Casey at the Bat" or whether it is still in copyright—but your publisher probably can. Or if someone wants a larger permission fee than you feel is reasonable, your publisher may be able to negotiate a better deal. Remember, your publisher wants your book to be just as big a success as you do and is always ready to supply assistance.

19

Introductions, Dedications, Prefaces, and Other Front Matter

19.1 *Front Matter—Putting Your Book in Context*

Hold front matter to a minimum if possible. Typical self-help/how-to readers are spooked by, or may skip over, lengthy front matter that includes a foreword, preface, introduction, acknowledgments, and other scholarly appurtenances. Professionals call this front matter because of where the material is found in a book. All a self-help/how-to book should need is a dedication, table of contents, introduction, and acknowledgments/permissions page. You may wish to include a preface if you think it will help the reader understand the text better; and by all means include a foreword written by an authority in your field if you can get one. But try to keep these sections on the short side.

19.1.1 The Front Matter Checklist

Use the following checklist when preparing your book for publication. The checklist includes, in the correct order, all the basic types of front matter. You won't need every one of these sections—but with this list, you won't omit anything important. Front matter can include the following:

☐ Title page

☐ Dedication

☐ Table of contents

☐ List of illustrations (if applicable)

☐ Foreword

☐ Preface or author's note

☐ Acknowledgments

☐ Introduction

☐ Permissions

19.2 *Title Page*

This page contains the full title—main title and subtitle—of your book, followed by your name and your coauthors' names if applicable.

19.3 *Dedication*

The dedication is where you dedicate your book to someone or some institution who helped inspire you along the way. Actually, you can include several people, if you want. Authors typically dedicate books to loved ones, friends, benefactors, the dearly departed, and others to whom they feel they owe a special debt of gratitude.

1. Type "Dedication" at the top of a page. Some publishers don't include this head, but you can include it for identification.
2. Type "To" and the name of your dedicatee.
3. If you wish, follow with a few short words of appreciation.

You'll find my dedication at the start of this book.

19.4 Table of Contents

The table of contents lists all the chapters in your book. It provides readers with an overview of your book and a quick way to locate your book's main divisions. You developed a tentative table of contents while outlining your book in Chapter 4. The list of chapters as they appear in the final book should accompany your completed manuscript when it is sent off for publication.

Also, send along an annotated table of contents. This is an expanded version of your chapter-by-chapter list. It includes all the headings and subheadings within the chapters.

Some publishers prefer the simple table of contents; others prefer the full annotated version. Include both with your proposal and the finished manuscript.

19.5 List of Illustrations

A list of illustrations is recommended only for books with a great many illustrations in which it would be helpful to the reader to have a guide for locating them quickly. It includes all illustrative material you use that is separate from your normal manuscript: photographs, drawings, charts, and other visual aids. Illustrations should be numbered when there are many of them. Use a combination that includes the number of the chapter and the illustration number. For example, the first three illustrations in Chapter 2 would be: 2-1, 2-2, and 2-3.

Numbering and listing illustrations
1. Type "List of Illustrations" at the top of a page.
2. Make two columns next to each other; title the first "Illustration #" and the second "Ms. Page #."
3. In the first column (the left-hand one), type the number of the first illustration to appear in your book.
4. In the second column (the one to the right), type the manuscript page number where the illustration appears.

5. Repeat the process with each chart, graph, and so on until finished.

When complete, your list of illustrations should look something like this:

Illus. #	Ms. Page #
1-1	3
1-2	5
1-3	8

There is no need to differentiate among charts, graphs, and illustrations here. It creates the scholarly look and adds nothing important to the reader's understanding. (For information on how to handle captions, see Section 20.6.)

19.6   Foreword

The foreword is usually a series of remarks about your book penned by some recognized authority within your field. A foreword is usually short, about four double-spaced manuscript pages. The author's name should come at the end, following the last line. The author's title or credentials follow on the line after that.

19.7   Preface or Author's Note

The preface or author's note is usually material intended to help readers make the most of your book. It includes:

- Why you wrote it.
- How to use it.
- Who it is for.
- Anything you have to say about yourself.
- Acknowledgments if they are short (see Section 19.9). Acknowledgments may also be contained in their own section.

Anything personal you have to say belongs here. Bear in mind, however, that some readers are turned off when an author writes too much about him- or herself. They want to know about things that relate to people like themselves.

19.8 Acknowledgments

The acknowledgments section is where you thank people and organizations that have rendered exceptional aid and assistance in writing your book. You may want to acknowledge any or all of the following:

- The staff of the local library, if they have been particularly helpful.
- Those who reviewed your manuscript and provided valuable suggestions.
- Anyone who loaned research material to you.
- Those who performed chores vital to the progress of your manuscript.
- Anyone you interviewed or consulted.
- Family members who put up with the disruption caused by writing the book.

Sometimes, when they are short, permissions and acknowledgments are combined on a single page under the heading "Acknowledgments and Permissions."

19.9 Introduction

The introduction generally contains material essential to understanding the text—historical perspectives or a dramatic overview of the importance of the subject.

19.10 *Permissions*

The permissions section is a list of every item for which you had to secure permission to reprint. (For information on how to secure permissions, see Chapter 18.) Sometimes, as with a photograph, you may have to include a credit line or copyright notice next to the photograph as well (see Chapter 20 for proper caption format). Use this simple format for your permissions sections:

1. Type "Permissions" at the top of a page.
2. Type the title of the first work from which you are quoting.
3. Type the name of the source's author.
4. Follow the name with the year the piece was copyrighted.
5. Add the name under which the work was copyrighted and the date of copyright renewal, if any.
6. Add the name of the party who granted the permission.

The result should look like this:

Grateful acknowledgment is made for permission to reprint from the following: *Low Man on a Totem-pole*, by Robert Benchley. Copyright 1936 by Popular Fiction Publishing Company; renewed 1966 Nathaniel Benchley. Reprinted by permission Doubleday Publishing Co. Last lines of the *Haiku* by Sharon Sucharitkul. Copyright 1993 by the Los Angeles Times, Inc. Reprinted by permission of the Ackerman Agency. "Long and Winding Road," by Paul McCartney. Copyright 1969 Apple Records. Reprinted by permission Michael Jackson, Inc.

20

Cross-References, Illustrations,
Charts, Tables, and the
Rest Made Easy

20.1 *What They Have in Common*

Cross-references (references to other chapters in your book) and
nontextual material such as illustrations, photographs, charts, and
tables all have one thing in common: They reference some part of
your manuscript to another part.

20.2 *Acing Your Way through Cross-References*

Cross-reference material when you are writing a section that is related
to material elsewhere in your book. You have seen it many times in
this and other books.

As always, keep it simple. In a few words, direct the reader to
the chapter or heading under which the information can be found.
Avoid page numbers if possible, as this will give your book the fatal
scholarly look.

Here are several effective approaches to creating useful, informal cross-references:

- "As we saw in the preceding section, the second step to health
  and fitness is twenty minutes of vigorous exercise every day."

- "The most important thing about building intimacy (Chapter 3) is understanding that we don't all perceive what being loving is in the same way."
- "Looking at a job's long-term advancement potential is far more important than short-term considerations like a larger salary (Chapter 3, "What Real Job Success Means")."

If you review the earlier pages of this book, you will see I have been using these formats for cross-referencing throughout.

20.3 *Illustrations, Photographs, Charts, Graphs and Tables, and Other Visual Aids*

Keep visual aids to a minimum. In self-help books, it's the message that counts. Unless absolutely essential, photographs, drawings, charts, and tables—and other visual elements that aren't part of the text itself—distract readers and add to the scholarly look. Besides, each visual piece complicates production for the publisher and drives up the cost of your book. Of course, when a point can only be made through a visual aid, by all means include it.

Illustrations are a necessity in many kinds of how-to books that guide readers step-by-step through the acquisition of physical skills. Among these are the following:

- Health and medicine
- Exercise
- Crafts
- Sports
- Hobbies
- Building and repair

In short, you are on safe ground using illustrative matter in any book oriented toward how-to.

One way to keep charts and tables from appearing academic and stodgy is to make them humorous. Many successful self-help/

how-to books contain light, funny, even cartoonlike charts, tables, and graphs to win readers. These can be the making of a bestseller. If your visual aids are more humorous than scholarly, go right ahead and use them. Readers will be delighted and so will publishers.

Fully explain each visual aid you use in the chapter where it appears. Tell readers precisely why it is there and everything they need to know to understand it.

20.4   Numbering and Referencing Visual Aids in Text

Citing illustrative material in your text is basically the same as cross-referencing chapters, sections, and subsections (see Section 20.2). Just follow these three simple steps:

1. When physically integrating visual aids in a book, the publisher's production department calls them "figures"—and so should you.
2. Number each figure by chapter and sequence, placing the chapter number first. For example, the first illustration in Chapter 8 would be designated "Fig. 8-1," the second would be "Fig. 8-2," and so on.
3. In the running text, set the figure number off in parentheses: (8-12).

This is how it would look in a sentence: "When making love in the lotus, or sitting, position (Fig. 8-12), breathe slowly and in the same rhythm as your partner to build harmony between you."

20.5   Marking Visual Aids for Publication

Write the figure number you used in your text in two places:

*   On the back of the visual aid
*   In the margin of your manuscript, next to the passage discussing it

20.5.1 Marking the Illustration

On the back of each photograph or drawing, print its figure number and the page of your manuscript in which it is first referenced—for example, "Fig. 6-8, p. 54."

Write these numbers in a very soft pencil or, better, a crayon-type marker. Keep them small but legible. Big numbers written heavily in ballpoint pen can press through the backs of drawings and ruin them for reproduction. Some editors even advise authors to print the figure number on a note and then tape it to the back of the illustration. This is a great help to them—and you—in case last minute renumbering becomes necessary.

20.5.2 Marking the Page

Next, when you reach the place in the manuscript where your visual aid belongs, type the figure number along with a brief description, and set it off with bars or a box, like this:

FIG. 2-9 HERE

20.6 *Captioning Visual Aids*

Put a caption below every visual aid you use. It can be as simple as the title of a chart, the name of a step, or a list of people in a photograph. Anything longer belongs in your text. Readers lose track of your ideas when they have to glance away from your main text for very long.

When you have to secure permission from someone else to reproduce a particular item you are using as a visual aid, that person may require an acknowledgment or copyright notice accompanying the photograph, drawing, or chart in question. If so, put it after your caption, in parentheses. (For more information on permissions and acknowledgments, see Chapter 18.)

The publisher considers your caption list a part of the manuscript and will use it for setting type for the captions, so follow the format guidelines below very carefully.

Formatting captions
1. Start a separate section of your manuscript, and label it "Caption List." This list of captions should accompany your completed manuscript when it is sent in for publication. Place it immediately following any cover letter and before the manuscript itself (see Section 17.3.2).
2. Double-space each caption, as you should all manuscript material.
3. Triple-space between each caption.
4. At the beginning of each caption, add the identifying figure number for the illustration it describes, plus the number of the manuscript page on which it is first referenced.

This is what your captions will look like once you put them in the proper form:

```
Fig. 5-12, p. 135.
Always keep your arms straight and elbows locked
when swinging a golf club.

Fig. 12-4, p. 211.
The above photograph shows the correct method
for stitching the edges of a quilt. (Illustra-
tion by Bjo Trimble.)

Fig. 8-3, p. 94.
Never pose someone against a cluttered back-
ground like the one above. This will distract
the viewer from your subject and confuse the
eye. (Photograph © ABC Archives.)

Fig. 21-6, p. 216.
The cast of the successful television program
The Big Clock. From left to right, Joe Blow,
Susan Smith, Norman Bean. (Photograph courtesy
Mary Jones.)
```

If some of your illustrations have captions and others don't, list each one anyway. This will help the production department avoid confusion when it is putting your book together. Just clarify which illustrations will not have captions, as follows:

```
Fig. 11-6, p. 150.
[No caption.]
```

20.7 Double-Check Your Cross-References

Ensure error-free cross-references—always double-check them when you review the final draft of your book. Make certain that if you have directed readers to the "Twelve Signs of Vitamin Deficiency" in Chapter 8, they really are in Chapter 8, not in Chapter 9.

No one's perfect. It's easy to make a mistake when juggling all the numbers involved in cross-referencing material and illustrative aids. It's even easier to make a mistake when you add or reorganize chapters. A final check will rectify any inaccuracies.

References, Bibliographies, and Recommended Reading Lists

21.1 Back Matter—All That Stuff at the End

Back matter, the material at the back of a book, is intended to further the reader's understanding of the book's subject. References, bibliographies, appendixes, resources, and indexes are all back matter.

After reading a self-help/how-to book, people often want to know where they can find additional information on the subject, groups of others with similar interests, and special publications and products. Gather all this material at the back of your manuscript, and put it in a form that readers will find simple to use and understand. Again, the best advice concerning back matter is to be sparing. Include only information that will help the typical reader.

In this chapter, we focus on references, bibliographies, and recommended reading lists. In Chapter 22, we finish up with appendixes, resources, and the index.

21.2 Footnotes and Numbered References

Most publishers agree that numbered references are generally not desirable in a self-help/how-to book. The purpose of references is twofold: (1) to acknowledge those sources from which you drew material for your book, and (2) to provide information that will enable the reader to find those sources if desired. A self-help/how-to book that requires many references is one that has borrowed too heavily from outside sources for a book that is supposed to reflect the author's own program or how-to methods. And most people are not going to check out your sources. Book reviewers aren't going to look them up, either. You also want to avoid having your book look too scholarly. In short, it's best not to have a back-of-book references section or numbered footnotes on the page.

If you do use sources, a bibliography, or better yet, a recommended reading section, should suffice (see Section 21.5). And in those places where you quote directly from a source and must give credit for the particular citation, the source can be given in the running text with full particulars (publisher, city, year) given in the bibliography. For example,

> According to eminent psychologist Dr. Milton White in his bestseller, *The Wonder Years*, "most children learn 90 percent of all the information they're ever going to know by first grade. After that, learning is simply a process of refinement."

If, however, you feel that a references section with numbered endnotes is necessary and important to your book, then follow the formatting described in Section 21.6.

21.3 Recommended Reading Lists

A bibliography is preferable to a references section, but if the books and publications you consulted could benefit readers, it's preferable to present them in a recommended reading list.

A recommended reading list is simply an informal list of books and publications that you recommend to your readers who want to know more about your subject. Because it's generally shorter and more focused, a recommended reading list is more useful to readers than a bibliography. You can make it more useful to your readers by adding a sentence or two following each entry, summing up what you find noteworthy about that book. When appropriate, include books on related topics. The recommended reading list for this book includes other books on writing plus references such as *Literary Market Place* and *Elements of Style*. If your list becomes more complicated, group books under topic headings. If you are writing about climbing the ladder to corporate success, you might arrange books under topic headings like "Networking," "Owning Your Job," "Career Transitions," or "Relationships in the Workplace."

Recommended reading lists have another advantage over bibliographies. You don't have to limit yourself to the books you drew on while writing. You are free to recommend any title you feel will be of value to your readers. For example, this book has a recommended reading list, rather than a bibliography, and it includes both types of books.

If you have appendixes, make your recommended list one of them ("Appendix B," for example). If your book doesn't have appendixes, simply head it "Recommended Reading."

21.4 Bibliographies

There are two approaches to formal bibliographies: the short form and the full form. Use the short form.

A short bibliography lists only books. It omits material from magazines, journals, and newspapers. The short form is really the most valuable, because back issues of magazines and scholarly publications are difficult for most readers to obtain. A full bibliography cites every publication you consulted, but such a bibliography is not preferred in a self-help/how-to book. When in doubt, discuss the matter with your editor.

If you do decide on an extensive bibliography and still wish to direct readers to books they might find useful, consider both a bibliography and a recommended reading list.

21.5 Formatting Bibliographies and Recommended Reading Lists

Arrange bibliographies and simple recommended reading lists alphabetically, by the authors' last names. If your recommended reading list has books under several topic headings, they should be alphabetically arranged within each heading.

Listing books
1. Start with the author's name (last name first).
2. Give the full title and subtitle (if any) in italic, or underlined.
3. List the city in which the book was published, followed by the publisher's name and the date of publication.
4. Place the entries in alphabetical order and you're done.

When you finish, your list should resemble this:

Bolles, Richard. *What Color Is Your Parachute?* Berkeley: Ten Speed Press, 1989.

Krippner, Stanley, ed. *Dreamtime and Dreamwork.* Los Angeles: Tarcher, 1990.

Maurer, Janet, and Patricia Strasberg, eds. *Building a New Dream: A Family Guide to Coping with Chronic Illness and Disability.* New York: Addison-Wesley, 1990.

If you are someone who absolutely will not be deterred from citing individual articles in your bibliography, use the following guide.

Listing articles from dated and numbered publications
1. Start with the author's name (last name first).
2. Give the full title and subtitle (if any) of the article in quotation marks.
3. Follow with the name of the publication in italic, or underlined.

4. List the full publication date given on the cover or contents page. Only when there is no day or month given should you supply volume and issue numbers.

This is the way a dated list should look:

Grunwald, Lisa. "Is It Time to Get Out?" *Esquire*, April 1990.

Lewis, Joy. "Fathers-to-Be Show Signs of Pregnancy." *New York Times*, 1 April 1985.

The format for a volume and issue number is as follows:

Trenholme, Irene, and Glen Greenberg. "Dream Dimension Differences during a Life Change." *Psychiatry Research* 5 (1992): no. 3.

For material from anthologies and collections, use this format:

Fiss, Harry. "Current Dream Research: A Psychobiological Perspective." In *Handbook of Dreams: Research Theories and Applications*, ed. Benjamin Wolman. New York: Van Nostrand Reinhold, 1979.

21.6 *References*

Only rarely do references enhance a self-help/how-to book's acceptance by discerning readers, reviewers, and colleagues—for example, if your book involves breaking-edge ideas and techniques drawn from primary research, or if it synthesizes extensive reading into new insights and approaches.

Leave reference numbers out of your book. They are rarely of benefit to typical self-help/how-to readers.

Here's how to keep both references and the popular look, while avoiding the use of distracting reference numbers in your text.

Formatting references

1. Type a reference list to go at the back of your book. List all references by chapter, giving the chapter number and title at the top of each chapter's entries.
2. Go to the first passage in your manuscript that requires a reference. Instead of typing a reference number for the first citation of your reference, type the number of the page where the passage appears.
3. After the page number, give the first few words of the passage in the text, followed by the name of the author, publication title, city of publication, name of publisher, and date.
4. Go to the next passage that needs a reference, and so on.

This approach eliminates scholarly looking numbers, while allowing curious readers to locate references with minimal difficulty. Properly done, your references ought to look like this:

p. 156 "Yuri Vlasov, the Russian weight lifter . . . ." Garfield, Charles, and Hal Z. Bennett. *Peak Performance: Mental Training Techniques of the World's Greatest Athletes.* Boston: Houghton-Mifflin, 1984.

If you cite a book or article more than once, after the first time just list the author.

p. 207 "Russian weight lifters prefer . . . ." Garfield and Bennett.

When referencing more than one book by an author, add an identifying word from the title after the author's last name. If you cite two books, say, by Mary Smith, *How Smart Women Succeed at Work* and *Career Strategies for Today's Woman,* your entries should read as follows:

p. 209 "Women who become winners . . . ." Smith, *Smart.*

p. 211 "Women build up, not . . . ." Smith, *Strategies.*

21.7 *Footnotes*

Avoid using footnotes at all if possible. The proper place to amplify an important point is in text. Footnotes are distracting and force readers to jump around in the text. They also give the scholarly look that you should avoid in a self-help/how-to book.

Use footnotes only to clarify a word, phrase, or concept likely to be unfamiliar to readers—and only when it would be too clumsy to explain in the text. Place footnotes in the back of your book, in a section of their own entitled "Notes" following the references section.

Formatting footnotes

1. Put a footnote number after any word or passage to be explained. Never use letters or number and letter combinations.
2. Give each footnote within a chapter a separate number.
3. Place footnotes in the back, in a chapter-by-chapter listing. Never do it at the bottom of a page.

22

Appendixes, Resources, and the Index

22.1 *Appendixes and Resources*

Turn vital information you want to share with readers—but can't seem to find a place for in any of your chapters—into appendixes. The venerable *Chicago Manual of Style* says that appendixes should contain all materials that are "not essential parts of the text but are helpful to a reader seeking further clarification," such as the following:

- Blank forms
- Checklists
- Graphs and tables
- A list of helpful organizations.
- An additional note to the reader or his or her loved ones
- A note to professionals
- Strategies for coping with day-to-day problems
- Legal or medical information
- Affirmations
- Resources
- Recommended reading (see Section 21.3)

The general rule of thumb is: If something doesn't fit anywhere else, and it's absolutely essential, start thinking appendix. When you have more than one appendix, letter them consecutively: Appendix A, Appendix B, and so on.

If you end up with four or more appendixes, if may be a signal that you are trying to make your manuscript carry too much weight for a self-help/how-to book. At that point, appendixes stop sounding useful and start sounding cumbersome and scholarly.

22.2   Resources—Aftercare for Readers

Showcase organizations and materials that can aid the reader's growth or knowledge. Readers who sincerely want to make use of what your book offers may desire to seek out sources of support and additional guidance. What's appropriate as a resource? Any or all of the following:

- Organizations that provide information.
- Support groups and networks.
- Audio and video aids.
- Help lines with 800 phone numbers.
- Web sites on the Internet.
- Companies that offer special products.
- Your own name and business address—and e-mail address if you have one—along with information about any courses or workshops you offer.

Formatting resources
1. Type "Resources" at the top of a page.
2. Skip several lines. If there is anything you want to explain about your resource list, type it here.
3. For each resource entry, put the name of the organization on the first line, the mailing address on the second, the city, state, and complete postal code on the third, and any additional remarks on the fourth. You can use the following (fictitious) example as your guide:

The Andrews Weightlifting Company
666 Beastly Drive
Crowley, PA 99999-9999
Equipment only. Catalogue: Free.

If your list of organizations is short and simple, it can be arranged alphabetically. If it is more extensive, group the organizations by state, type of service offered, or whatever is appropriate.

If you list more than one type of resource, arrange each type under its own heading (such as "Organizations," "Products," or "Services"). If there are subgroupings within each group, by all means give them their own headings, too. For instance, under "Organizations," you might list "Businesses" and "Hobby Groups" or, under "Products," you might have "Publications," "Audiotapes," and "Videotapes." Should these lists become extensive, start each on a new page and head it as a separate resource.)

If you plan to include descriptions of products and services, format the entry in encyclopedia style:

The Andrews Weightlifting Company, 666 Beastly Drive, Crowley, PA 99999-9999. Make a fine line of products. Their Complete Work-Out Kit is probably the sturdiest available at any price for home use.

22.3   The Index—Locating Key Points

The index is the section at the very end of a book that gives the page numbers on which people and subjects mentioned in the text can be found. Ninety-nine percent of the time, you will need an index in a self-help/how-to book. If you believe an index will not benefit readers, however, discuss the matter with your editor, who is in the best position to judge.

Your publisher will offer to hire a professional indexer to do the work (it's written into every book contract). Accept the offer. They will deduct the cost (typically less than a thousand dollars) from your future royalties, but it won't cost you a penny out of pocket or from your advance. (And, incredible as it seems, you don't have to pay it back if your book should fail to earn royalties.) Only if you have some overriding reason should you spend your own time preparing an index.

Generating and formatting the index
If you decide to prepare your own index, you could start listing possible entries from the final edited manuscript. But you will not be able to enter page references until you receive your typeset page proofs, which publishers provide authors for correcting. The publisher will usually provide you with a set of proofs just for indexing, and depending on the book and the publisher, this may be a "revised" or corrected set in case any of the page numbers changed during correction.

1. Review your book.

2. Make a list of the following:

   Any subject a reader might need to look up.
   Every person quoted or mentioned.
   Every book quoted or mentioned.

3. Review your list. Is anything missing, or could anything be dropped? Under what key word would the reader most likely look for each topic listed?

4. Type the key word, phrase, or name, followed by the number of the page (or pages), where it is mentioned:

   Meditation, 36, 74, 252
   Mertz, Fredrika, Ph.D., 11
   Healing Power of Humor, The, 44, 256

5. To cross-reference another entry in your index, use this format:

   Medicine, allopathic. *See also* Physicians, allopathic, 56, 224, 229

6. If a subject has subdivisions, include subentries:

   Relaxation techniques, 122
   > meditation, 178, 184
   > yogic breathing exercises, 126

7. Alphabetize your index when you are done.

8. Double-check all entries to make sure the page numbers are correct. This is a good idea even when you are using a computer. It will help you discover any places where you or your computer might have made an error.

Appendix A

Recommended Reading

Publications That Can Help

If you want to know more about the business or craft of writing, you will find all the books listed here invaluable aids and references. I accumulated mine over the course of several years. Not everyone is in a position to run right out and spend several hundred dollars on new books all at once. So to get you started, I'm going to list the three books I think should be in the library of every writer, beginner or veteran.

The Indispensable Three

Chicago Manual of Style, The. Chicago: The University of Chicago Press, [current edition].
    More than indispensable, the bible of the publishing industry, and the primary authority for just about everything: punctuation, numbers, technical names and terms, foreign words, copyediting, abbreviations, manuscript preparation, proofreading, a glossary of publishing industry terms, and more.

Herman, Jeff. *Insider's Guide to Book Editors, Publishers and Literary Agents*. San Francisco: Prima Publishing, [current edition].
    Thousands of listings. Along with valuable information on

manuscript preparation, proposals, submissions, how-to slant for various categories, and much else budding authors need to know. May be the single best comprehensive one-volume value for someone writing their first book.

Strunk, W., Jr., and E. B. White. *The Elements of Style*. New York: Macmillan, [current edition].
The classic, and still the best, guide to clear and effective English.

Valuable Resources

Begley, Adam. *Literary Agents: A Writer's Guide*. New York: Poets and Writers, 1990.
Guides you through the ins and outs of agents, plus it tells where to find them and what their areas of specialty are.

Bunnin, Brad, and Peter Beren. *The Writer's Legal Companion*. Reading, Mass.: Addison-Wesley, 1993.
The latest on how to avoid legal pitfalls. In-depth coverage of case histories, copyrights, permissions, contracts, and much, much more.

Carroll, David L. *How to Prepare Your Manuscript for a Publisher*. New York: Paragon House, 1988.
The title says it all. A must-have for beginning authors.

Contracts & Royalties: Negotiating Your Own. New York: Poets and Writers, 1989.
Everything you need to know about this all-important subject—whether you have an agent or do it yourself.

Cool, Lisa Collier. *How to Write Irresistible Query Letters*. Cincinnati: Writer's Digest Books, 1987.
Highly recommended. The author shows you how to draft letters that will have agents and publishers begging to read your book proposal.

Editors of *Webster's New World Dictionary*, The. *Webster's New World, Misspeller's Dictionary*. New York: Prentice-Hall Press, 1983.

A must even in the day of computer spell-checking programs, if, like me, you can misspell a word so completely that you baffle the most sophisticated software.

Literary Market Place, R. R. Bowker Co., 121 Chanlon Road, New Providence, NJ 07974. Issued annually. Slightly over $100.

You only need to update with a new copy every five years, so the price tag isn't that bad on a yearly basis. What you get is a cornucopia of indispensable information:

- Complete listings of all large and most small book publishers, with addresses, editors' names, company sizes, and types of books they publish.
- Complete listing of every major and most minor literary agents, addresses, their requirements, and kinds of books they specialize in.
- Thousands of listings for editorial and ghostwriting services, lecture agents, literary prizes, clipping services, public relations firms, stock photo agencies, printers, and dozens of other categories.

Publisher's Weekly, 249 West 17th Street, New York, NY 10011. About $50 for a six-month sample.

The glossy trade magazine of the publishing industry. Will give you real insight into the business itself, current trends, forthcoming books in your subject area, hot agents, covers, and everything else. You will get your money's worth alone from the annual "self-help" issue (focusing on self-help publishers, editors, and books), and the special triple-sized Fall and Spring Announcements issues previewing 90 percent of the year's forthcoming books.

Seidman, Michael. *From Printout to Published*. New York: Carroll and Graf, 1992.

An excellent insider's guide, written by a veteran editor who has worked for a number of major publishing companies. Tells you everything you need to know about selling and marketing your book—from beginning to end of the process. The chapters on working with publishers to promote and market your book are highly recommended.

Shaw, Eva. *Ghostwriting: How to Get into the Business*. New York: Paragon House, 1991.
    You can't get along without this one if you are ghostwriting a self-help book or working on your book with a ghostwriter. The only book of its kind.

Appendix B

Organizations That Can Help

The following organizations provide valuable services for members and nonmembers. You may wish to contact them for information on membership and the benefits they offer. Your city and state probably also have writers' organizations whose members can be an important source of insight and assistance.

American Medical Writers
    Association
9650 Rockville Pike
Bethesda, MD 20814

American Society of
    Journalists and Authors
1501 Broadway, #1907
New York, NY 10036

The Author's League of
    America
234 West 44th Street
New York, NY 10036

National Association of
    Science Writers, Inc.
P.O. Box 294
Greenlawn, NY 11740

The National Writers Union
13 Astor Place, 7th Floor
New York, NY 10003

About the Author

Jean Marie Stine, a professional editor and author specializing in self-help books, has worked for such publishers as Putnam, St. Martin's, Houghton-Mifflin, and Jeremy Tarcher. Her writings have appeared in such periodicals as *The L.A. Weekly, Los Angeles Guide, The Washington Post,* and *Movieline.* Jean's most recent books are *It's All in Your Head: Amazing Facts about the Mind* and *Double Your Brain Power: Using All of Your Brain All of the Time.* Ms. Stine currently serves as Director of Publications for the International Foundation for Gender Education.